Setting Sail

Marigot Bay, St. Lucia, on the Windward and Leeward Islands. (*The Moor*

SETTING SAIL

How to Buy a Boat and Cruise the World on $300 a Month

Lawrence Taylor

Icarus Press
South Bend, Indiana
1981

Setting Sail
How to Buy a Boat and Cruise
the World on $300 a Month

Copyright © 1981 by Lawrence Taylor

Manufactured in the United States of America.

Icarus Press, Inc.
Post Office Box 1225
South Bend, Indiana 46624

1   2   3   4   5   6   7   8   84   83   82   81

Library of Congress Cataloging in Publication Data

Taylor, Lawrence, 1942-
    Setting sail.

    Bibliography: p.
    Includes index.
    1. Sailing. 2. Sailboats. 3. Sailboat living.
I. Title.
GV811.T36   797.1'24   81-7085
ISBN 0-89651-700-4   AACR2

Contents

Preface

Setting Sail: How to Buy a Boat and Cruise the World on $300 a Month can act as a guide to achieving a happier and healthier life, cruising the oceans of the world. It is not an instruction manual on how to sail, nor is it an attempt to teach the intricacies of yacht design, navigation, or seamanship. The reader will find many books covering these and related subjects in the bibliography at the end of this book—and he or she should read many of them carefully before embarking on a blue-water cruise.

What this book *does* attempt to do is two things. First, the book will convince you, the reader, that it is not only *possible* to buy your own boat, but that it is really quite a simple matter to retire aboard that boat for the rest of your life—regardless of your present financial or family situation. I hope you will see that almost anyone is capable of realizing his dream of sailing the world's seas with his own boat, free of all the demands and penalties that go with living in an increasingly polluted and pressured environment. The only requirements are two: desire and common sense.

Second, this book will take you, step-by-step, from where you are now to where you want to be: experiencing the freedom and pleasures of sea voyaging. It will explain the economic realities of boat life and will outline a simple and realistic plan whereby you can own your own boat in a year or less—and have enough money set aside to finance your cruising for a long time to come. If you should ever run short of money, a chapter will discuss how you can earn a living aboard your floating home, no matter where you are. It will explain some of the considerations that go into choosing a boat, will present some of the better models currently available, and will set forth some of the intricacies of buying that boat. You will then be led through the various preparations necessary to a successful life afloat and, finally, will be briefly exposed to the primary cruising areas and routes of the world.

There are hundreds, probably thousands, of books that will teach you how to sail, shoot stars, repair engines, survive storms, recognize weather fronts, and so on. None of them, however, will show you how to get aboard that boat bound for the far horizon in the first place.

This book will.

Part 1
The Cruising Life

If a man does not keep pace with his companions,
perhaps it is because he hears a different drummer.
Let him step to the music which he hears,
however measured or far away.

1

A New Way of Life

The mass of men lead lives of quiet desperation.

Tom Phillips is thirty-nine years old, a successful insurance salesman with a lovely wife, two handsome young children, and a large home in a fashionable suburb. It is Monday, the start of yet another week, and it begins with the jarring sounds of rock music blaring out from Tom's bedside clock radio. Stunned, still grasping for reality in the premorning darkness, he staggers to the bathroom and begins the same ritual he has undergone almost every day he can remember. His head aches from too many cocktails at the Pearsons' last night, and he quickly downs a couple of aspirin.

Kate, his wife, also fights her way through the haze of sleep as she fumbles through the closet for her bathrobe. She wakes the children, then goes downstairs and turns on the coffee maker. The kitchen radio is turned on; the announcer is advising his public that stocks are down, pork bellies are up, and gold is holding its own.

Still in a semitrance, Tom walks into the kitchen and quickly drinks down a cup of life-giving coffee. His mind begins to focus as he sits at the breakfast table, and Kate pours him a second cup. He opens the newspaper, quickly reads of three new murders, a terrorist hijacking, and another local politician caught with his hand in the till; one of the murders, he notes with little feeling, took place in full view of dozens of spectators—all of whom chose to pretend it simply was not happening. He turns to the financial section, learns that the cost-of-living index for the month has again reflected double-digit inflation. He nervously studies the stock-market reports, then feels a wave of relief as he learns that more of his stocks increased in value the previous day than declined. The sports page gives him more good news—the local professional basketball team won again, though the star has announced his intention to quit unless he receives 1 million dollars a year.

A third cup of coffee, a polite kiss for Kate and each of the kids, and Tom gets into his late-model station wagon and drives off toward the freeway. The car radio blares more news into his ears as he edges his way toward the freeway; the air will be relatively safe to breathe today, the announcer advises his audience, but small children and older citizens should avoid play or physical exertion. As always, the freeway is jammed with bumper-to-bumper traffic, a virtual parking lot for as far as the eye can see. Tom looks apprehensively at his watch, then tries to compute whether he will make the office in time for the regional sales manager's meeting; if he misses this one, it will reflect in his efficiency file.

Tom inches the car forward, stops, goes forward a few more feet, then again hits the brakes. A car in the next lane suddenly swerves into the short space between Tom and the car in front of him. Tom feels a surge of anger. He hits the horn. The driver makes an obscene gesture, continues working his way into the small space in front of Tom, daring him to hit his car. Tom feels the anger spreading, growing into something like hate. His heart is pounding, pressure is welling up in him, straining to burst free.

An hour later, Tom walks into the office—ten minutes late. He already feels exhausted from the wars on the freeway and grabs yet another cup of coffee to jar him into awareness. He enters the conference room, mumbles an apology to the frowning boss, and sits down. He is only half-aware of the droning voice of his boss, pacing back and forth in front of a large financial chart. He tries absently to loosen the collar and tie around his neck; they only seem to constrict ever more tightly.

When the meeting is over, Tom goes to his desk and reads through the pink messages that are already stacking up. One by one, he begins to return the calls. An auto collision claim . . . form W 24, in triplicate. An expanded benefits of life insurance . . . form 2101A, four each and one to the main office. A business client, canceling a group policy . . . form AB27, triplicate, with accompanying memo of explanation. The phone becomes heavy as another business client advises him of a burglary during the night—the third this month . . . form 2722, and recommendation of cancelation.

Three hours later, Tom puts the telephone down, grabs his coat and enters an elevator on his way to a luncheon appointment with an insurance prospect. The elevator has only four people in it, but each is studiously pretending that no one else is there; Tom, himself, feels a vague discomfort in the silence.

The elevator door opens, and he walks out of the building into the streets. His eyes smart, and he feels a shortness of breath as the heavy smog accosts him; it is a sunny day, but the sun is only a gray-brown blur behind the layers of industrial pollutants that thicken the air. He pulls out his pack of cigarettes for the sixth time that morning, lights up, and then draws in the soothing smoke; he coughs, but the calming effect is something he needs desperately.

He maneuvers his way through the throngs of lunch-hour foot traffic, enters the restaurant. Sam is waiting impatiently for him at a table, looking at his watch. Tom greets him apologetically, then joins him in a martini. After a brief glance at the menu, Tom orders a dietetic special; his doctor has advised him that he is overweight, and his cholesterol count is too high. The two men talk about the basketball game the previous evening, then switch to the subject of insurance. They order another round of martinis as Tom continues trying to convince Sam that he needs an expanded coverage in his policy.

Lunch over, and a sale successfully made, Tom rushes back to his office feeling a slight sense of well-being from the drinks. He lights his seventh cigarette as he enters the office, then sits down to begin dictating an endless succession of letters and memos to a bored, gum-chewing secretary.

By five o'clock, Tom is exhausted and experiencing another headache. He chews a couple of aspirin on his way to the darkness of the subterranean garage. He looks nervously from the corners of his eyes at the darkened corners of the parking structure; a number of robberies have taken place here within the past couple of months, but the police are too short-handed to do anything about it. He lights another cigarette as he gets into the car, slowly maneuvers the station wagon up onto the street level and out into the ever-present battle of traffic.

After ten minutes of stop-and-go, he glances at his fuel gauge. Nearly empty. My god! he thinks to himself, I filled it just a couple of days ago! But he will have to stop to fill up the big wagon again. Another thirty dollars. And he remembers reading something in the papers about the Arabs jacking the price of oil up again—for the second time this year. Tom feels a rage building again, a dull controlled fury.

Safely back home, Tom takes off his tie and shoes and settles back into his favorite chair in front of the television set. His two kids are already glued to the TV and only barely acknowledge his arrival. He asks them how school was, and they silence him with a cursory "OK" without taking their eyes from the set.

Kate announces that dinner is ready. As always, the kids beg to have dinner served in front of the TV. And as always, Tom relents; the family eats their dinner together in total silence, four sets of eyes riveted to the glowing screen.

Three hours later, Tom and Kate climb the stairs toward their bedroom. Tom has a half-empty cocktail in his hand, and he experiences an urge for one last cigarette. He feels sluggish, drained, and his head still aches slightly. He looks at Kate; his wife's face is expressionless but for a faint hint of boredom. He thinks about the bills that have piled up on his desk, bills that have to be paid—the mortgage, car payments, car insurance, life insurance, telephone, the electric company, two credit card companies, gas, cable TV, and on and on. The checking account has to be balanced, and their stock portfolio reviewed. He decides to deal with them tomorrow.

With mumbled good nights to one another, Tom and Kate turn out the lights and get into bed. Lying in the darkness, Tom escapes into his favorite fantasy: sailing off into a beautiful sunset, bound for the South Pacific. Only sixteen more years, he thinks to himself—sixteen years to retirement and a nice pension. Sixteen years, and then he can begin to do what he wants. Sixteen years, and he can begin to live.

Next year, Tom will have his first heart attack.

Mack is also thirty-nine years old, also has a wife—named Jean—and also has two young children. Like Tom, Mack was an insurance salesman with a dream. Unlike Tom, however, Mack decided to realize his dream before his heart canceled his ticket. Unlike Tom, Mack and his family decided to live *now*.

It is the same Monday morning that Tom faced. Mack rises from his starboard bunk to the slight rocking of the boat as it surges through the ocean's broad swells. The gentle sounds of water rushing along the hull greet him, and he hears the cry of a seagull as it hovers somewhere above the boat.

He steps across the cabin to the galley, pours himself a cup of coffee from the pot that has been left for him by Jean. The hot

12

bitterness tastes good in the cool morning air, and he stretches his muscles. He had only been asleep for four hours—his was the midnight-to-four watch at the wheel—but he feels relaxed, refreshed, looking forward to another interesting day.

Mack climbs up the companionway and looks out of the cabin into the cockpit. Jean grins, her hands casually on the yacht's wheel. Their little girl is playing with the cat, laughing as she feeds him a flying fish that had landed on board during the night. Mack looks around, spots their boy sitting near the bow, his legs dangling over the side. He is pointing at the water ahead, shouting enthusiastically. There in the ocean, just a few feet ahead of the boat's surging bow, are four or five blue-grey porpoises. They are playfully frolicking back and forth across the bow, challenging the boat to a race across the deep royal blue waters.

Mack takes a deep breath, feels the clean, fresh air at the bottom of his lungs. A gentle breeze whisks through his hair, and the salty tang in the air smells indescribably good. The sun is just clearing the razor-sharp horizon in the distance, spreading its warm glow toward the little vessel, welcoming it, bidding it to continue on its journey.

Mack sits down in the cockpit next to Jean. They talk for a while, both excited about their expected landfall that evening. Finally, he takes the wheel, and Jean goes below to prepare breakfast. The young boy comes back, excitedly telling his father all about the gamboling porpoises. They talk about porpoises and whales, while the little girl continues playing with the cat.

Scrambled eggs, bacon, toast, and fresh-squeezed orange juice are soon served on the cockpit. Under the powder blue skies and the spreading warmth of a rising sun, Mack and his family eat their breakfast. Each member of the family is hungry, and the food seems to taste especially good in the fresh sea air, with foaming salt water gurgling by just beyond the reach of a hand.

Eating together, the family talks about what they had seen on their watches during the night, and what they are expecting at their new landfall. Another tropical island, but each is different, each has something unique to offer.

Breakfast finally over, Mack sets the self-steering vane and releases the wheel. He goes below and brings out the charts and navigational gear. Carefully, he plots the distance and direction made good during the previous night's passage. This places him only forty-five nautical miles from the reef opening to the island. They would arrive, therefore, in about nine hours. He double-checks his computations, making a mental note to double-check his "dead reckoning" with a noon sun sight with the sextant. He can't afford to make mistakes; the safety of his family depends upon his knowing exactly where they are and avoiding the hidden reefs in this part of the world. But he is confident—a confidence built upon self-reliance, upon self-knowledge.

Mack grabs some of his tools and climbs back up onto deck. Jean is conducting her daily classroom, teaching the two kids most of the subjects they would have learned back in the city; right now they are going over an arithmetic textbook she obtained from an educational supply company. Mack grins to himself, feeling a sense of joy that he could give his children so much more of an education than other parents could. His kids learn math, reading, writing, and history—but they also learn about porpoises and flying fish, about celestial navigation and diesel mechanics, about foreign lands, strange cultures, and new tongues. They learn about people and places and the natural wonder of things. Most importantly, they learn about themselves.

He looks at each of the two children again. They are both trim, sun-tanned, and filled with life. They are healthy, and they are happy.

Mack goes forward and begins to work on the turnbuckle of the starboard shroud. Corrosion has set in, and the wise course is to replace it before a sudden storm places more stress on it than it could handle. Under the warming sun, the deep blue water rushes past him, Mack laboring in his shorts, his bare back and legs open to the ocean's breeze. It is hard work, and he sweats, but it is a good feeling. It is honest work, and there is a pleasant feeling in knowing that you exist—and conquer whole oceans—without help from anyone.

Lunchtime comes quickly, and the family gathers in the open cockpit for a real treat. The boy had set out a spring line over the stern, a feathered jig tied to the end of a hundred yards of fishing line. And an hour before lunch, he had gleefully hauled in a small mahi-mahi—a brilliantly colored South Pacific dolphin fish. He quickly cleaned and cut the fish into steaks (his dad had taught him how), and his mom cooked up four of the slices in a pan of diced onions and peppers. And it was delicious—fresh dolphin under the blazing tropical sun.

The afternoon finds Mack repairing tears in two of the sails with his canvas-saving kit. With a sail spread over his bare legs, he can lean back against the mast, breath in the fresh ocean air, and feel the sun baking his bare shoulders. He looks back toward the cockpit and watches as Jean renews her classroom efforts. He is always surprised at how much more enthusiastic the kids are about learning now than they had been back in the city. Maybe it was having the world for a classroom; maybe it was having your own teacher all to yourself; maybe it was just a sharpened sense of living.

Suddenly, the boy jumps up and points to the horizon ahead, yelling excitedly. Mack looks forward. Sure enough, barely visible on the distant horizon is a low-lying island—right where he expected it to be. Four hours to landfall.

After the excitement dies down, Jean brings out the geography books and the kids begin to learn all about this new land they are about to visit. Mack walks around the boat, double-checking the anchor and line, preparing the dinghy for use, and bringing out the papers that would be needed to clear customs and immigration. Once again, he studies the harbor chart, memorizing the opening in the submerged coral reef that surrounds the island, as well as the two shipwrecks inside the reef.

A half-hour before sunset, the little sailboat slowly drifts through the opening in the reef. Mack is aloft in the shrouds, directing Jean at the helm as he keeps a watchful eye on the passing coral. Seeing coral is more difficult with the sun low in the sky, but the opening is wide and the coral near the surface.

The boat glides silently through the lagoon. Everyone in the family is transfixed by the beauty of the island—lush green mountains, with ribbon-like waterfalls spilling down into a crystalline bay. Two other sailboats are at anchor in the lee of the largest mountain, near a ramshackle pier. Mack takes over the helm and guides the boat to an area near the two vessels, then once again goes through the ordered drill of dropping anchor that Jean and the kids perform almost automatically. Anchor dropped slowly, slack, engine reversed, anchor set. No second anchor necessary here. Over the side with the dinghy, just as the local officials come along in their motorboat.

An hour later, and the sun is set. The flaming reds, oranges, and yellows of the tropical sky are beginning to recede, as Mack and his family chat over dinner in the cockpit. The talk is of the adventures in store for tomorrow on the island—new people, new places, new experiences. An awning has been spread above them over the boom in case of a sudden squall, but the warm evening breeze flows gently through unimpeded. Tonight, the family will sleep on deck and in the cockpit.

After dinner, a young man and an older couple from the two neighboring boats row over for an evening drink. The young man is sailing alone around the world; the older couple are simply drifting from place to place as the mood strikes them. But everyone speaks the same language; everyone shares in the same lifestyle, the same dream. Strange, Mack thinks to himself, but he couldn't imagine himself and Jean having a good time with people outside their own age and income group back in the city. Yet, none of that seems relevant here.

When the friendships have been cemented and the stories told, the guests leave for their own floating homes. Alone now, Mack and Jean sit in the cockpit under the stars. The tranquility of the anchorage seems to seep into them, lulling them into a sense of peacefulness. Water laps softly against the hull, and the sweet scent of tropical flowers is in the air. The moon is almost full, illuminating the entire bay with a silvery sheen.

2

It Can Be Done

I know of no more encouraging fact than the unquestionable ability of man to elevate his life by a conscious endeavor.

Fine, you say, it all sounds very charming—sailing off into tropical sunsets, leaving the high-pressured world behind. But there are only two things wrong: I can't even row a boat, much less sail around the world; and I don't have a nickel in savings, but I do have a stack of bills piling higher each day.

Let me tell you a story—a true story—about a Frenchman by the name of Bernard Moitessier. Monsieur Moitessier was an itinerant fisherman in Viet Nam, without money or family, but with a dream—a dream of sailing the oceans of the world in his own boat, free like the albatross that soared in the skies above him. He painstakingly saved every penny he could, until he had enough to buy a rotting old Chinese junk that was due to be scrapped. The little boat was deemed unseaworthy for continued use in coastal trading, but Moitessier grabbed her from the salvage men and set sail alone on the open seas, bound for the distant horizon. In the middle of the Indian Ocean, the junk was leaking so badly that she began sinking faster than he could bail. Finally, he had to dive over the side and patch up the hull with make-shift materials ripped from the boat. In this floating wreck, Moitessier sailed into the teeth of the monsoon season for eighty-five days—without any navigational instruments. Not surprisingly, the old junk ended up wrecked on the shores of Mauritius Island.

Moitessier worked for three long years on Mauritius, taking odd jobs and doing anything that would earn him a *sou*—but always with the same dream in his head. During these three years, he spent most of his spare time building another boat with his own hands out of wood scraps and whatever else he could find. At last, the boat was ready for the seas and Moitessier set out once again for an undefined goal somewhere on the other side of the world.

The Frenchman rounded the Cape of Good Hope and crossed the Atlantic by himself, fighting periodic gales. He had almost nothing in the way of modern equipment and had to struggle with the helm by himself day after day! Overcome at last by fatigue, he was again shipwrecked—this time in the Antilles. His second boat was, like the first, a total wreck.

But Moitessier still did not give up. Stranded in a strange land, with $60 in his pocket and with no employment available to foreigners, Moitessier decided to return to France where he could earn some money to build a bigger and better sailboat to conquer the world. But how to get to France with almost no money? Simple: Build a boat out of paper!

Moitessier then proceeded to buy enough wood for $10 to construct a makeshift frame for the hull. He would cover this frame with a layer of scrap newspapers, and plaster that with a layer of pitch. Then another layer of newspapers, followed with more pitch—and so on until enough layers were present to result in a hull that would keep the water out. He would finish the hull with a covering of torn jute sacks sewn together, plastered with yet more pitch. The 35-foot sailboat would have no deck, no cabin, and only a rudimentary mast and rigging system—but it would sail!

Soon after beginning the project, however, Moitessier had a stroke of luck. A Norwegian tanker had pulled into Trinidad needing a replacement for a deserter from its crew. The Frenchman happily signed on, and in the following months was steaming all over the Atlantic. Finally, he reached Hamburg, where he jumped ship and made his way to France.

In Paris, Moitessier met and fell in love with Françoise; the two were soon married. But this did not stop Moitessier from continuing his vagabonding ways. He simply included his new wife in them.

Moitessier looked around for the highest-paying employment he could find, and landed a job as a salesman for a pharmaceutical company. Of course, he immediately began building another boat—this one, a 39-foot steel-hulled proper yacht, with old telephone poles for masts. The boat looked like a giant lobster, bulging at the sides and painted a bright red all over. This vessel, he swore to himself, would not be smashed to pieces on a reef!

Françoise had two young children, and they were sent off to schools so that she could accompany her new husband on his adventure. Wisely, she realized that there was no way to hold him back from his dream, and so she joined in it.

On October 20, 1963, Moitessier and his wife departed Marseilles for the open ocean. They sailed across the Atlantic to the Caribbean, on through the Panama Canal, to the Galapagos Islands, and then to Tahiti. After spending time lazily visiting the Polynesian island groups, the couple decided to return to France to rejoin the children. Moitessier took the hard way, of course, sailing south around fearsome Cape Horn, dodging icebergs and fighting mountainous seas. Finally, on March 29, 1966, the bright red ketch slipped back into Marseilles.

19

But domestic tranquility did not suit Moitessier. He began to feel the itch to be at sea again, white sails pushing him on toward ever-changing horizons. In 1968, he heard of a race sponsored by the London *Sunday Times*. The *Times* was offering 5,000 pounds sterling and a golden globe to the winner of a single-handed sailboat race around the world. The idea excited the Frenchman, and he immediately began preparing his "red lobster" for another extended cruise. He said good-bye to his wife and the children and sailed from Toulon to Plymouth to start the race. He left Plymouth on August 22, 1968—two months after the start. He sailed south, around the Cape of Good Hope, and east on toward Australia—taking the dangerous route in the "Roaring Forties." On he pressed, through the South Pacific, then around the terrible Cape Horn and into the Atlantic. He headed north now, on the last leg of the race—and, surprisingly, near the lead in his homemade boat!

Then, suddenly, Moitessier realized that the race itself was meaningless. It was the oceans, the sea birds, the playful porpoises, the mysteries of nature, the knowledge of solitude—these were what mattered. Despite being in contention for the prize, Moitessier wrote out a message to the *Sunday Times*, placed it in a small canister, sailed it with a slingshot onto the deck of a passing freighter. The message was very short: "The Horn was rounded February 5, and today is March 18. I am continuing non-stop towards the Pacific Islands because I am happy at sea, and perhaps also to save my soul."

Moitessier did continue on alone—on around the Cape of Good Hope once again, on south of Australia again, through the Roaring Forties, on into the South Pacific. This represented a total voyage of one and a half times around the world—the longest single-handed voyage in history!

Do you still think it can't be done? Bernard Moitessier was chronically broke and had a wife and two children to support. But he also had *desire*. That, and a little common sense, carried him a long way.

Let's take a closer look at the two biggest objections of frustrated men who would sail the seas: *knowledge and money*.

Knowledge. Most men dismiss the possibility of cruising as a way of life because, well, they don't know how to sail! What such men don't recognize, of course, is the obvious: Bernard Moitessier once didn't know how to sail, either, and there was a time in the life of Sir Francis Chichester, a grocer by trade, when the sight of a sailboat was a completely strange one. No one is born with the ability to sail; even the greatest mariners had to learn how to steer a small boat first, how to tack, how to jibe. It makes as much sense to give up the idea of ever driving a car simply because you don't know how. Sailing, like any activity, must be learned. Fortunately, it is a fairly simple task—simpler than, say, flying. And a hell of a lot cheaper and more fun!

Give me any man or woman, and I can give you a competent sailor in a matter of months—or even weeks. It doesn't matter whether he or she is a farmer in Kansas, an accountant in Atlanta, or a truck driver in Los Angeles. If an ocean is not nearby, a lake will do; the principles are the same, and the demands of ocean sailing can be learned and adapted to later. The important thing is to get started by learning the basics; the rest will come in time.

So the first thing to do is to sign up for a beginning sailing class. These can usually be found rather inexpensively—often through the city or county recreation department; the YMCA, community colleges, and other organizations also offer courses on how to sail. If a private sailing school is nearby, these can be very good though more expensive; the instructors make their living at it. At the same time, some private schools are subsidiaries of some yacht broker; these schools are often merely a "front"—used to back up offers of free sailing lessons with the purchase of a yacht. If you have trouble finding a sailing class in your area, contact the Coast Guard or the local boating auxiliary.

The beginning class will teach you the proper nomenclature of the boat—*starboard, port, sheet, windlass, boom, shroud*, etc.—and the basic handling of a small sailboat. You will learn the points of sail, sailing close to the wind, running, tacking, jibing, changing sails, docking, and so on.

At the same time, you should obtain the latest edition of Chapman's voluminous *Piloting, Seamanship and Small Boat Handling*. Study this book. It is a treasure of knowledge about rules of the road, coastal navigation, boat rigging, marine equipment, sailboat handling, and a thousand other useful things. Armed with this book, you will soon know more about boats and sailing theory than most weekend sailors. Of course, sailing cannot be learned in a book, no more than driving or flying can: you've got to get out there and *do* it. But there is a whole lot to deep-water cruising that can be learned in one of two ways: the hard way or the easy way. Take the easy way, and start learning the ways of the sea now through reading. It's painless, and it's fun.

The beginning sailing class will take maybe a month of meeting on weekends. Having completed that, and having studied Chapman, proceed on to the next step: advanced sailing techniques. With any luck, there will be further classes available in your area for learning more complex skills. You will learn anchoring techniques, man-overboard recovery, steering without a rudder, racing techniques, and many other valuable skills.

21

If no such classes are available, try to find a sailing co-op or club that has small boats for hire; most of these have programs for group sailing, and the advanced skills will soon be learned from the more experienced members of the club. If no such club or co-op exists, hang around the docks where sailboats are kept and try to make friends with boat owners who would like to have another crewmember aboard. If nothing else, place an ad or notice on the bulletin boards of yacht clubs and anchorages, offering your services free. Guaranteed: Try hard enough with the right attitude and you will succeed in becoming a knowledgeable sailor!

Now that you have gained the *knowledge* of basic sailing, you must gain *experience*. It is one thing to know the rudimentaries of handling a sailboat; it is quite another to sail her around the world—through storms and reef-infested seas. Of course, there is no real way to learn how to deal with storms and reefs other than actually to do it. And, of course, anyone who waits to have that experience before he departs on his world cruise will never leave the dock. You can, however, do two things: read about other mariners' experiences and broaden your own experiences with sailing.

The more familiar you become with sailing within the limitations of your geographical and economic situation, the more likely you will be able to handle a boat under the most severe of conditions. Again, become involved in the nautical community near you: join clubs, volunteer to serve as crew. Experience is, after all, simply a product of time and opportunity.

At the same time that you are becoming more and more familiar with the "feel" of a sailboat, you should expand your reading beyond

Chapman. And this can really be fun: How many armchair adventurers are there that read about blue-water voyages for the vicarious thrill of it? The fact is that there are very few books written by voyagers that will not teach you many things learned from hard trial-and-error. Read Eric Hiscock's series of books for a particularly valuable education; Hal Roth's and Bob Griffith's books are further examples of adventures packed with sage advice. Make no mistake: The knowledge passed on in these books is invaluable and will make your future cruising life infinitely easier and more pleasurable. You are painlessly benefiting from hard-earned wisdom. Besides, there will be times during your "learning and earning" period when you may lose sight of just what you are working so hard for; the adventures in these books will remind you.

22

Now you are becoming more proficient at sailing, and you are learning through books and/or classes about seamanship. But there is more to cruising than boat handling. Now is a good time to enroll in a class on coastal and celestial navigation. If no classes are offered locally, the skills can be largely self-taught through books. A sextant will be necessary, but perhaps one can be borrowed; Davis Instruments offers a cheap plastic version for around thirty bucks—perfectly suitable for learning on. Knowledge in other areas of cruising can also be picked up now in the evenings with a book: oceanography, meteorology, boat maintenance, diesel mechanics.

About this time in your development as a blue-water sailor, you should be fishing for invitations on weekend cruises. If you are on the "1-Year Plan" discussed later in this book, you will already be living aboard your own boat. Either way, short cruises will teach you many of the things that will prove valuable on the longer cruise. Different anchoring situations, changing weather conditions, equipment breakdown—these all contribute to your experience as a mariner, and the knowledge gleaned from them will undoubtedly make you a better cruising sailor.

So if you can't sail, learn! It's easy, it doesn't cost a lot, and it's mighty fun.

But what about that second roadblock: money?

Again, there is nothing that can stop you from retiring aboard that boat and sailing the oceans of the world—if you want it badly enough! No matter how sick your present financial picture is, it *can* be done. In a later chapter, we will examine the "1-Year Plan"—a simple, realistic procedure by which you can start from scratch and, within one year, own your own sailboat and have a healthy "stash" laid away to finance many years of cruising.

In yet another chapter, we are going to take a close look at the many ways that a cruising skipper and his family can make a living by part-time work wherever he happens to find himself. None of this work entails abandoning the cruising life; in fact, many of these "jobs" use the boat and your cruising skills to earn money.

So read those two chapters, and then sit down and ask yourself if you can "afford" to retire aboard your own sailboat. Take out a pencil and paper, and take stock of your financial assets and liabilities. Applying the principles of the "1-Year Plan," project the feasibility of such a "dream." You will find that it is not only attainable, but attainable within the near future. And one of the nice things is that while you are earning the initial grubstake you are also learning the skills necessary to carry out the dream.

Money problems may prove a temporary detour, but it is not a dead end. Any financial problem can be overcome, if you want something badly enough. At the very worst, bankruptcy is a possibility—offering a clean slate; in two years, that bankrupt can be on his way aboard his own boat. And it is doubtful you, the reader, are anywhere near bankruptcy.

Money is not a block; it is an excuse. If Bernard Moitessier can take on the ocean with a paper boat and an empty pocket, then *anyone* should be able to overcome financial problems. It is simply a question of *desire*.

Again: Read about the "1-Year Plan." Read about making a living while cruising. Then ask yourself if you could do it.

But I have three kids, you say. And I'm fifty years old. And my wife doesn't want to go sailing. And it's dangerous. And . . .

Wait a minute. Are these excuses? Ask yourself one more time how badly you want to cruise the seas aboard your own sailboat. If you want to badly enough, you *will*.

One of the finest examples of a blue-water mariner living today is Eric Hiscock. This Englishman has written a number of books about cruising that are absolute gold mines of information. These works are based upon his own personal experiences in sailing the seas of the world, and the experiences are considerable. He has circumnavigated the globe *four times* and in the process was awarded the prestigious Blue Water Medal of the Cruising Club of America. He has cruised to just about every corner of the globe and continues to do so to this day. Oh, yes, Eric Hiscock was born in 1905. And his wife, Susan—who is only a few years his junior—has accompanied him on all his voyages as first mate. The Hiscocks have been living aboard now for over thirty years and are currently on their fifth circumnavigation of the world!

At the other extreme, consider Robin Lee Graham. This enterprising fellow took off on a tiny 24-foot sloop and singlehandedly sailed his way around the world. He was seventeen years old when he left Los Angeles' harbor.

Children? There is no healthier environment for a growing child than that offered by a cruising boat. Clean air, physical activity, learning self-reliance, seeing strange lands and people, experiencing nature to the fullest—can there be a better classroom anywhere? Children are cruising with their parents in boats all over the world. There is nothing novel about this. And they love it. In fact, kids seem to take to the blue-water lifestyle more readily than adults—perhaps because they are more adaptable and less impressed with society's traditional values and standards.

In the next chapter, I will discuss the considerations of a family afloat. Enough for now to assure you that cruising is not just for the single man: It is a lifestyle that very readily embraces both the wife and children.

Too dangerous, you say? Sure, there is danger involved. And if avoidance of danger is the paramount consideration in life, then life is best spent safely tucked away in a warm, soft bed. Yet the risks of cruising have been greatly exaggerated. A well-found boat and a knowledgeable and alert skipper will see years of long-range cruising without serious mishap. Few experienced cruising sailors are ever lost to the ocean. Of course, anything at sea is possible, but the chances of death or serious injury are infinitely greater if you simply drive onto a freeway or try to walk across a street.

Self-assessment time again. If risk is the paramount consideration to you, then you are probably not the cruising type—not that cruising is unduly dangerous, but simply because you are more concerned with safety and security than freedom and adventure. A concern for the well-being of one's wife and children is understandable and praiseworthy, but a simple fact remains true: The more you try to ensure against the hazards of life, the less you will experience of it. The individual with a deep-water sailor's heart will not want to huddle in his cocoon; on the contrary, he will want to reach out, explore, see, touch, feel. He will not want safety; he will want freedom.

This is not to say that ocean voyaging is necessarily dangerous. At sea, the danger lies primarily within oneself: One's own knowledge and abilities are his protection against mishap. Far more accidents occur at sea because of ignorance or inattention than because of uncharted reefs or overpowering storms.

Once again, it *can* be done. It requires only desire. And a little common sense.

3

The Family Afloat

Why should [men] begin digging their graves as soon as they are born?

The objection most frequently raised by would-be cruisers is, "But I have a wife and two kids." The presumption, of course, is that ocean voyaging is a man's game—a dangerous enterprise with no place for women or children.

That attitude is archaic. Granted that circumnavigating the globe in the days of Joshua Slocum was a risky venture, one that required a lot of courage and physical stamina, blue-water sailing today is no more dangerous—and probably a lot less—than braving our cities' freeways. Assuming a skipper with common sense, a willingness to learn, and a seaworthy boat, cruising is a safe and sane way for the entire family to live.

The times have changed. The cruising sailboats of today are simply better boats than those available to wayfarers of fifty or a hundred years ago, and the equipment is more advanced. Fiberglass, ferrocement, steel, aluminum—these materials have made sailboats stronger, faster, and more seakindly. New designs and materials have converted a deep-water yacht into a safe, comfortable greyhound. Technology has given the cruising boat long-distance transmitter-receivers, depth finders, knotmeters, radar, computerized navigation, self-steering devices, graphite masts, power windlasses, self-rolling sails, pressurized hot water, refrigeration, stereo—not to mention instant navigation by satellite. An individual can make his boat as loaded with these gizmos as he wants. Of course, no amount of equipment—no matter how sophisticated—is ever going to be a substitute for a knowledgeable skipper. But the point is this: The boats and equipment of today make deep-water cruising a *potentially* safe way of life. The materials to give safety and relative comfort to your family are there; you need only add some learning and the all-important common sense to ensure their well-being at sea.

26

Fine, you say, but neither my wife nor my kids are particularly excited about selling the home and taking off like sea gypsies. So what do I do? Give up on the dream? Or take off by myself, single handed?

First, a word about single-handed ocean sailing. It has been done—by many people. Today, there are even special transoceanic races for single-handers. But solo voyaging takes a very special kind of person. If you are the kind of individual who prefers your own company to that of others, who finds pleasure or meaning in being completely alone for weeks on end, and who has tremendous physical stamina and mental strength, then perhaps you would do well alone on the empty seas. There are such men—Bernard Moitessier, Vito Dumas, Josh Slocum, Harry Pidgeon, Sir Francis Chichester, Alec Rose. But for the vast majority of people, single-handed cruising would be a lonely, fatiguing, miserable experience. The isolation from human companionship can weigh heavily, and the physical and mental demands are terrific. As a noted world cruiser, Bob Griffith, once wrote: "A single-hander must be ready to die, scared or not, each time he lays down his head to sleep; self-steering rigs keep no lookout."

Nor do you give up on your dream. Initial family reluctance is only one of many obstacles between you and a better way of life on the seas. If you fold simply because your wife or kids are hesitant to change the status quo, then you probably do not have the fortitude and determination it takes to become a good sailor. Or perhaps that family resistance is just an excuse—an easy way out of facing a new challenge? An excuse to continue on in what you know has become a deadly dull, unhealthy—but comfortable—rut? You should understand one simple fact: *If you do not begin now with your plans to cruise, you probably never will.*

You deal with this understandable initial resistance from the wife and kids very simply: You get them *involved*. You get them involved in sailing, involved in cruising, involved in your dream. The kids will probably be easy. There are few youngsters who do not take to blue-water sailing, if they feel an important part of it. The wife will be more difficult . . . but not impossible. Most women who are happily cruising today were initially against the idea. It is, perhaps, in the nature of man to wander and in the nature of women to want a hearth. But the number of couples and families successfully living aboard their boats attests to the fact that women *can* find joy in a floating home, and can even, in time, prefer it to their previous conventional lifestyle.

Maybe the best initial approach to the problem is to meet some cruising people and strike up a friendship. It should be easy; you will find that most "liveaboards" tend to be natural, open, and friendly, and relatively unaffected and unimpressed with possessions, appearances, and other things that normally keep people apart. Then introduce your wife to them. Let them—and particularly the feminine half of the team—talk to her. Let her see for herself their way of life, hear for herself how happy the wife is with the lifestyle.

Then get her *involved*. Perhaps your new friends will take you both out—and the kids too—on a day sail or even on a longer cruise. If you are not fortunate enough to meet such people, get your wife involved in sailing as a sport. Take her out on sailboats; sign her up for sailing lessons. She will find that sailing small boats is fun and easy, once she gets the hang of it. If she does not get "hooked" on sailing, at least she will have lost her fear of it. The same goes with the kids. Get them out there on Sabots or Lidos or Lasers or whatever; with most kids, this will be pretty easy.

Once the family is into sailing, ease them into local cruising. Charter a boat for weekend "gunkholing," camping out on beaches with barbecues in the sand. Cruise in company with another boat or two. There are few wives and fewer children who would not take to such family mini-vacations.

Now that they are into coastal cruising, it is just a matter of time before the idea of blue-water cruising becomes acceptable. Again, however, the key to acceptance is *involvement*. Once the tentative OK has been won, don't make the common mistake of trying to do everything yourself, trying to be all things. Give each member of the family some responsibility, some real role in the coming adventure. Don't simply relegate your wife to the role of cook; let her learn navigation or first aid, or put her in charge of giving the children a formal education at sea. Try to abandon your concepts of the kids as helpless dependents. At sea, they can be very useful, as you will soon learn—standing watch, steering, acting as bow lookouts, performing simple maintenance, changing sail, and so on. So get them involved now.

One good way to do this is to assign everyone a field of expertise: Each child is told that the learning of some skill or knowledge is his or her responsibility and that the family will depend upon that expertise on the voyage. For example, the eight-year-old will be assigned the job

27

of learning all about marine cooking—the problems of cooking at sea, the equipment necessary—and of acquiring recipes suitable for use in the galley (there are dozens of books with recipes specifically for cruising). A secondary field of expertise may be marine biology— learning all about the animals that live in the sea. The eleven-year-old can be assigned the role of meteorologist; it will be his job to learn all he can about the weather—what to look for in the skies, how to read weather charts, how to predict wind conditions. His secondary field may be geography—finding out all about the different places and people that can be visited in the boat. You may assign yourself the job of learning to work on diesel engines or acquiring the arts of coastal and celestial navigation. And the wife might get the task of learning how to repair sails, or learning the rudiments of dental and medical care at sea.

You will find that this assignment of roles or specialties has a threefold benefit. It gets the family involved, giving each of them the feeling that they are an important part of the planned voyage (and they are). It creates a source of skills and knowledge that can be used to advantage at sea; unlike on land, each member of the family can make important contributions to the common well-being aboard a boat. And, finally, learning skills offers a great form of entertainment.

You will probably be dealing with a period of time—perhaps a year—during which you and your family will be scrimping and saving to get up enough money to buy a boat and have enough left in the kitty to finance a few years of cruising. During that period, you will be cutting back drastically on normal expenditures, such as for entertainment. Yet learning these new skills is exactly that— entertainment. You will find that your spare time, and that of your wife and kids, will be enjoyably spent planning the cruise and acquiring these new skills and areas of expertise. Rather than going out to dinner or to a movie, your family will be learning navigation, first aid, oceanography, meteorology, diesel mechanics, and so on. It is more educational, more fun, and it brings the family together. There are few things more enjoyable than preparing for a world cruise . . . unless it is actually being on the cruise.

A word about bringing the family together. Cruising can be a very unifying experience. Each member is contributing in a very real way, and the family experiences the adventure as a team. There will be adverse times that will be faced together and times of "heaven on earth" that will be shared together. But cruising can also be a very divisive experience, if it is permitted to be. In all too many cases, a family that sets out on a world cruise learns to hate one another before the first month is past. Certainly, the cramped conditions of a boat can cause problems: Even the most compatible of individuals can come to detest one another when jammed together in a kitchen-sized enclosure for weeks at a time. But the secret here is to ensure that each person has a space and time to himself or herself, and not to stay on the move for too long.

There is such a thing as the "territorial imperative"; humans need space. Each member of the crew should have his own bunk, his own storage space, and a part of the boat for his particular work. Equally important, each member needs time to himself—time away from the rest of the family. No matter how much that member loves the others in the family, he or she needs distance and isolation periodically. A perfect solution for this is the standing of watches. Each member of the family who is old enough will be assigned a watch during which time he or she will be alone at the helm. A four-hour watch from, say, midnight to four A.M. will do wonders for the psyche.

At the same time, you should not try to stay at sea for too long. Make short passages, if possible, and remain at anchor for extended periods of time. Let you and your family stretch yourselves physically and mentally by going ashore and wandering around freely. Everyone needs it.

If there are still problems of compatibility at sea, you should perhaps consider the following factors suggested by a cruising expert, Thomas Colvin:

1. Has the wife adjusted her conventional views and values yet?
2. Would coastal cruising be more acceptable than cruising for long distances at sea?
3. Is the boat of a wrong type or size?
4. Are finances causing tensions?
5. Is the boat properly equipped to deal with the needs of the family?
6. Are difficulties communicating with friends or relatives causing problems?
7. Is there difficulty adapting physiologically or psychologically to local food and customs?
8. Does any of the family simply not enjoy travel or seeing new places and meeting new people?
9. Is boat maintenance becoming intolerable?
10. Have you simply had a run of old-fashioned bad luck—gales, sickness, equipment failures, etc.?

Identifying the source of friction between family members is the first step in eliminating it.

All well and good, you now say, but my kids are in school: I can't just yank them out and put an end to their education.

Let us be very clear about two facts of life. One, there is absolutely no better education for a child than to be able to cruise to foreign lands, to experience foreign cultures, to live with nature. Two, you and your wife probably represent—at least potentially—more effective teachers than the ones your kids currently have in school.

The world is the cruising child's classroom. Every day is a new experience. He learns responsibility and a sense of self-reliance from his duties aboard the boat. He learns about the weather, about the oceans, about sea life and the birds above. He explores new countries firsthand, not in books, and meets children and adults of strange cultures. He does not *read* about Samoans or Papuans or South Africans, he talks with them, eats with them, laughs and plays with them. Is there a better way for a child to learn of the world he lives on? And is there a healthier environment, physically or mentally, in which to learn?

True, the child must receive a formal education as well. He must be taught reading, writing, and arithmetic—as well as science, history, and so on. But consider for a moment the education your children are now getting. Is it really that good? Are the teachers that proficient and that dedicated? Is your child getting enough individual attention, or is he lost in an overcrowded classroom? What makes you think that you and your wife could not effectively teach your child in a one-on-one situation?

A recent article in *Reader's Digest* reported that the general level of competence among teachers has seriously deteriorated. A large percentage of teachers today, the article disclosed, "simply have not mastered the basic skills in reading, writing and arithmetic that they are supposed to teach." The horror stories of teacher incompetence are increasing, but consider the not uncommon story of a child who brought home the following note from his teacher: "Scott is droping in his studies he act as if he don't care. Scott want pass in his assinment at all, he had a poem to learn and he fell tu do it." Still think you cannot do as well?

So how do you go about learning to teach your children and setting up a proper curriculum for them? The first thing to do is to read books about teaching—books that will teach you to teach. Your local library or the nearest university's department of education should be able to supply you with appropriate books. The following list should be particularly helpful to choose from in learning how to give your kids a good formal education at sea:

Fostering Intellectual Development in Young Children,
Kenneth Dann (Teacher's College Press)

How to Raise a Brighter Child, Joan Beck (Trident Press)

How to Instruct (U.S. Department of the Air Force)

Big Rock Candy Mountain: Resources for our Education, Samuel
Yanes (Delacorte)

Teaching Children to Read, Lillian Gray (Ronald Press)

Teaching the Child to Read, Guy Bond (Macmillan)

The Years before School (3d ed.), Virginia Todd (Macmillan)

Guiding Children's Language Learning (2d ed.), Pose Lamb
(William C. Brown)

Teaching Young Children, Roma Gans (World Book Co.)

Parents are Teachers, Wesley Becker (Research Press)

Teaching Montessori in the Home: The Pre-School Years,
Elizabeth Hainstock (Random House)

Teaching Montessori in the Home: The School Years, Elizabeth
Hainstock (Random House)

Montessori for Parents, Dorothy Fisher (Robert Bentley)

Learning the Three R's (2d ed.), Gertrude Hildreth (Educational
Publishers)

*Contemporary Pre-School Education: A Program for Young
Children,* Shirley Moore (John Wiley & Sons)

Give Your Child a Superior Mind, Siegfried Englemann (Simon &
Schuster)

Social Studies for Children (7th ed.), John Michaelis (Prentice-
Hall)

Helping Your Child Learn the New Arithmetic, David Engler
(Criterion Books)

A Handbook for Geography Teachers, Robert Gabler (National
Council for Geographic Education)

Let's Play Math, Michael Holt (Walker and Co.)

Exemplars for the New Social Studies, Frank Ryan (Prentice-Hall)

Teaching Secondary English, John De Boer (McGraw-Hill)

Child Development, Arnold Gesell (Harper)

The Reading Improvement Handbook, John Rosenblum
(Washington State University)

Basic Reading Skills for Junior High School Use, William Gray
(Scott, Foresman & Co.)

Basic Reading Skills for High School Use, William Gray (Scott,
Foresman & Co.)

Let's Read Series, George Murphy (Holt, Rinehart and Winston)

Building Your Vocabulary, John Gilmartin (Prentice-Hall)

31

This is, of course, only a partial list—a few of the hundreds of books available to teach yourself to teach. But the point is clear: The materials are available.

Once you learn the rudiments of education, you will select suitable textbooks to take along on the boat. Along with these, you might consider including a good dictionary, a world almanac, a world atlas, and a condensed version of an encyclopedia, such as Collier's or Columbia. Another very valuable educational tool is the old "Great Ideas Program" of the *Encyclopaedia Britannica*. Consisting of ten small volumes, the set offers a heck of an advanced education in science, government, math, law, literature, and philosophy.

If you still have little faith in your own abilities to select and administer a curriculum, you should look into a formal program set up by an educational institution for such purposes. These consist of either correspondence courses or "independent study programs." The correspondence courses are fairly self-explanatory: The child follows the instructions in his materials and forwards homework and/or tests to the educational institution for grading and further instructions. The benefit of this is that the child receives a professionally designed curriculum and obtains formal credit for completing courses or grade levels. The problem is one of time and distance; maintaining mail communication with the institution can be very difficult aboard a cruising sailboat. In any event, the correspondence course must still be administered and supplemented by the parent.

Another method is the independent study program. Many child actors in Hollywood use this method when filming. Basically, this consists of a program offered by some school districts whereby the parent acts as the teacher but follows a syllabus set up by the school and uses the school's materials. The child is later tested—perhaps by mail—and given formal credit. You must, of course, find a school district offering such a program and willing to enroll your child in it.

A number of colleges are now offering independent study programs as well. It is possible in some of these colleges to actually obtain a degree through independent study (i.e., without ever setting foot on the campus). A quality example of such a program is that offered by the University of California (mailing address: Independent Study, University of California Extension, 2223 Fulton Street, Berkeley, CA 94720). The following excerpts from the University's Extension catalog will give a feeling for such a program:

> You are urged to begin no more than three courses simultaneously, enrolling for additional work after some progress has been made in the first three courses . . . .
> Students residing outside the U.S. should allow as long

as three months for delivery of syllabi sent via surface mail: you are urged to pay for air mail delivery of course materials. Independent Study will extend the usual one-year completion period, on request, to compensate for the time enrollees relying on foreign surface mail have waited for the arrival of course material and texts . . . .

There is no academic penalty for failure to complete an Independent Study course, and terminated enrollments do not appear in transcripts . . . .

In addition to assignments listed in each course description, most courses require supervised final examinations; a few require mid-course examinations as well . . . . Students residing in other states or outside the United States may have final exams monitored by secondary school principals, college or university faculty administrators, librarians, U.S. Embassy or Consular Offices, education officers at U.S. military bases, or other persons specially approved in advance.

Credit earned through Independent Study may be applied toward adult degree programs now being offered throughout the United States. These programs—many of which are new and unusual—vary in format from the New York Regents' Degree programs (for which there are no residence requirements) to part-time programs toward which a limited number of Independent Study courses may be accepted.

If a member of your family is interested in gaining college-level credit for various subjects while cruising, he or she should be aware of the "College-Level Examination Program" (CLEP) and the "American College Testing Program" (ACT). These programs offer examinations on various subjects; if the person being tested is successful, he is granted credit for completing the subject course. If, for example, you learn Spanish or French on your trip, you will be given course credit if you can pass an exam. Information on CLEP can be obtained by writing to The College Board, Western Regional Office, 800 Welch Road, Palo Alto, CA 94304; info on ACT can be had by contacting ACT, Box 168, Iowa City, Iowa 52240.

Two other addresses you might want to contact for information are:

International Institute
P.O. Box 99
Park Ridge, Illinois 60068

American School
Drexel Avenue at 58th Street
Chicago, Illinois 60637

33

The International Institute offers correspondence courses for kindergarten through the eighth grade, and the American School has high school courses. Also, you can get in touch with the National Home Study Council (1601 18th Street, N.W., Washington, D.C. 20009) for a directory of accredited correspondence schools throughout the United States.

Do not be overly impressed with various secondary or primary school programs simply because they offer formal credit for completing a course or a grade level. If you continue on cruising permanently, the child can obtain a high school diploma from many schools simply by taking an examination known as a "general educational development" (GED) test. If you have done your job as a teacher, he will probably score higher on it than he would have had he stayed at home and received a traditional education. If you decide to end your cruising before your child has completed his high school education, whatever school district you settle down in will probably want to give him or her a placement test (i.e., an examination to determine the child's educational development and the proper grade in which he should be placed). His placement will depend on what he has *learned*, not on what certificates or diplomas he has been given.

The rules vary, of course, from state to state and from school district to school district. You should contact your local district or state authorities to determine their regulations and procedures. They may also be helpful in designing an educational format—a curriculum tailored to the particular needs of your children for the coming years at sea. If nothing else, they may be able to suggest textual materials for your use in teaching them.

The family, then, is not an obstacle to finding a happier, healthier life cruising the oceans of the world. The truth is that the family is an invaluable *asset* to achieving that goal—each member contributing his or her share. Although as a unit independent of society once at sea, the family needs one another and relies upon one another aboard a boat. And this very fact brings the members of that family closer together.

34

4

Testing the Water—
Cruising Schools and Chartering

*I went to the woods because I wished to live deliberately, to front
only the essential facts of life, and see if I could not learn what it had to
teach, and not, when I came to die, discover that I had not lived.*

Individuals thinking about embracing a new lifestyle cruising the
oceans of the world aboard their own boat often have the same
question: How do I know it's really for me? This is a valid question
and one that should be asked by anyone contemplating such a drastic
change of lifestyles. Cruising is a beautiful way to live, but it is not for
everyone. . . . fortunately! So how do you find out if cruising is for
you? How can you determine whether you are adaptable to that kind
of life *before* you sell your house, buy a boat, quit your job, and burn
all your bridges behind you?

Fortunately, there is an easy way—chartering. You simply rent a
boat for a week, two weeks, or a month—and experience first-hand
what it is like to live aboard and cruise. Of course, this will be a limited
experience: Most of the drudgery of boat maintenance and repair will
be done by the charter company that owns the boat. And long passages
will probably not be possible; the boat will already be based in good
cruising waters and must be kept within a certain range of its home

port. Still, a couple of weeks behind the helm should give you a pretty good idea if this is the kind of life you want to lead.

There are basically two kinds of chartering arrangements: bareboat and crewed. The bareboat charter involves the renting of the boat only; the customer sails the boat himself. A crewed charter, on the other hand, means you are renting the boat and also hiring a professional sailor to skipper it. Each has its advantages. The bareboat charter is, of course, less expensive; on the other hand, a skipper has extensive local knowledge of the waters and can teach you quite a bit about sailing and cruising. Eventually, you are probably going to want to "go it alone"—as you should. You will want to take that 32-foot cruiser out and sail her through the Virgin Islands with only your wife and kids aboard; only then will you really know the independence and responsibilities of cruising.

No chartering company is going to turn one of their expensive yachts over to a novice, however. They are going to want proof that their investment is in good hands. Generally, they are going to require that you submit the names of references who can verify your knowledge and skills. Even then, most charters will quite reasonably insist on a brief test of your abilities, in the form of a "check-out" sail before your charter begins. If you seem to know how to navigate, anchor, and handle a boat, you are on your way. And once you have qualified with one chartering company, you are usually accepted by others without much question.

Fine, but how do you qualify in the first place? There are three primary ways. First, try a crewed charter to begin with and learn all you can from the skipper. If you become proficient enough at sailing with him, he will eventually certify you for bareboating. Second, take classes from sailing schools which offer instruction in navigation and cruising skills; they will not only give you experience but will serve as a reference. Third, and least expensive, get your sailing experience from sailing with friends. If you don't know anyone who owns a cruising boat, look around the marinas and yacht clubs; boat owners are always looking for unpaid crew to race or cruise with.

Sailing Schools

Before we get further into chartering, then, let's take a look at schools which offer specialized courses in navigation and cruising. Some of them, by the way, will issue certificates upon the completion of their courses which indicate you are qualified to charter bareboat; most charterers will accept them, but will still require a "check-out."

Top: Learning the techniques of cruising. The excellent Annapolis Sail School offers (*Annapolis Sailing School*) Above: Learning courses in basic and advanced sailing, racing, coastal navigation at sea. (*Annapolis Sailing* cruising, chartering, and coastal and celestial *School*) navigation.

Two of the biggest and best-known are the Annapolis Sailing School and Steve Colgate's Offshore Sailing School. The Annapolis Sailing School (P.O. Box 3334, Annapolis, Maryland 21403; 800/638-9192 toll free) has established branches in San Diego, California; Lake Geneva, Wisconsin; Charleston, South Carolina; St. Petersburg, Florida; St. Croix, U.S. Virgin Islands; and St. Lucia, West Indies. Each location has a slightly different format and curriculum, but most offer everything from beginning sailing to liveaboard cruising. They hold classes in coastal navigation and piloting, as well as celestial navigation, and even offer a five-day class specifically designed to qualify you for bareboating. Most interestingly, Annapolis has learn-while-you-cruise courses, which offer the best of both worlds: You cruise the Virgin Islands, the Florida Keys, or the West Indies, while the skipper teaches you the techniques of blue-water sailing, anchoring, navigation, or whatever. Not a bad deal. The cost? Prices as of 1981 were, for example, $175 for coastal navigation, $125 for a one-weekend beginners' course, $325 for the bareboat qualifying course, $600 for a ten-day learning cruise of the Florida Keys or the Dry Tortugas, $800 for a nine-day cruise through the Virgin Islands, and $950 for a deep-water voyage from Annapolis to the Virgins (or return). The instructors are Coast Guard-licensed, and the boats range from Chrysler 22s to Pearson 26s on up to the O'Day 37 and Newport 41. Annapolis Sailing School is a pretty good operation, offering the chance to learn the skills of sailing and at the same time experience something of the cruising lifestyle.

Steve Colgate's Offshore Sailing School (820 Second Avenue, New York, New York 10017; 800/221-4326 toll free) is another reputable outfit that can teach you to sail, to cruise, and to bareboat. The school has six branches: Captiva Island, Florida; Irvington, Virginia; Martha's Vineyard, Massachusetts; Bar Harbor, Maine; Tortola, British Virgin Islands; and Bermuda. They offer a combined beginning-intermediate "learn to sail" course taught aboard 27-foot Solings, which takes a full week and costs (in 1981) $395. They also have a "learn to cruise" course which also involves a week of instruction and sailing, covering such subjects as tuning the boat's rigging, coastal navigation, docking and anchoring, handling the boat under power, and the mechanics of engines, stoves, and heads. The cost for the course is $425 and is offered in conjunction with hotel packages at some of the branch locations.

There are other sailing schools that teach the arts of cruising, of course; Annapolis and Colgate's Offshore are only the best-known and most extensive in their offerings and locations. A quick check with your local National Red Cross chapter, Coast Guard, U.S. Power Squadron, Coast Guard Auxiliary, or community colleges—not to mention the yellow pages—should unearth some local schools, though they will probably not offer cruises.

Chartering

Back to chartering. There are dozens of commercial companies which offer bareboat and/or crewed charters. A quick look at the display ads toward the end of *Sail, Yachting,* or *Cruising World* magazines will give you some indication of the variety of such commercial offerings. Write to a few of them; study and compare the brochures and price lists they send you. Some of these are pretty slick outfits—and expensive—with large fleets of boats and their own marinas. Others are smaller operations, with prices that reflect a minimal advertising budget. Yet others are merely business firms acting as agents for the private owners of the boats being chartered. Any of these can be the source of a good sailing experience—or a miserable one. There are good chartering companies, and there are bad ones. If you can, ask the charterer for the names and addresses of people who have sailed with them before; if they will not comply, forget them.

Costs will vary from charterer to charterer, depending upon the type of sailboat, the charter company, the location, the season, and the supplies that are included in the deal. Adding a skipper or crew will, of course, increase the price. Very, very roughly, you should expect to pay somewhere in the neighborhood of $500 a week to bareboat a 27-footer, and more like $1,000 for a 35-footer. Add (roughly) $50 a day for a skipper if bareboating is out. Obviously, costs can be reduced on a per-person basis if you charter in partnership with another family or even two. They can also be reduced—and the hassles of crowds be cut in half—by cruising in the off-season. The Caribbean is the most popular chartering location in the world, and it is packed during the winter with sailors escaping the cold climates of the Northeast and Midwest. Yet the best sailing conditions are often in the other months, and the costs are less.

The British Virgin Islands are a favorite cruising area, being visited here aboard one of Tortola Yacht Charters' C&C 39s. Chartering is an excellent way to find out whether cruising is for you.

Before leaving home, you should understand exactly what is ahead of you. You should have a copy of the chartering agreement and understand your obligations and responsibilities. You should know what type of boat you have contracted for, and exactly what provisions are being supplied by the charter. Normally, the chartering company will provide ice, stove fuel, linens, cleaning supplies, first-aid kit, tool kit, dishes and cutlery, flashlight, pots and pans, navigational equipment, and charts of the cruising area. You, on the other hand, are usually expected to bring such items as food, booze, soap, insect repellent, sun tan lotion, skin diving gear, binoculars, and fishing tackle. Some boats come fully provisioned with food and liquor at additional cost; although expensive, this does save time you would normally lose by having to shop for these things near the marina.

Before you jump into a contract with one of the big chartering agencies, though, you might want to consider doing business with a private boat owner. This usually—though not always—means getting a boat for less money; you aren't paying for the display ads and big overhead. At the same time, the reputation of individual boat owners is harder to discern: He could be an honest fellow with a solid, spit-shined boat, or he could be a flake with a rotting tub. When you write him, ask the fellow for a photograph of the boat (he is probably not going to have a brochure like the big boys) as well as the names and addresses of recent customers.

A modern charter service center—The Moorings, on Tortola in the British Virgin Islands.

Again, a good source for private owners who charter their boats is at the back of the sailing magazines—in the classified ads, under *Charters*. There are dozens of them in each issue, ranging from day sailers to luxury yachts. If you don't want to cruise in one of the popular areas represented in these advertisements, you should check your local newspaper (or, if you are landlocked, the paper of the nearest coastal or Great Lakes city), or ask around the local marinas or yacht brokerages. You can often work a pretty good deal this way—for as little as half what a chartering agency will charge.

The following represent some of the better-known but less expensive charter companies arranged geographically. It is not a comprehensive list and certainly does not constitute a recommendation by the author. But they are well established and will provide brochures and information upon request. Most offer bareboat but provide crew or skipper if needed; many have learn-to-cruise or learn-to-sail programs. Prices indicated are for weekly rates, unprovisioned, as of late 1981.

California

Aventura Sailing Assn.
35102 Del Obispo
Dana Point, CA 92629

Has 100 boats, sailing school. Chartering requires joining their club.

Pacific Charter Co.
555 N. Harbor
Redondo Beach, CA 90277

Has boats in Redondo Beach, San Diego, Dana Point, and Newport Beach.

Pacific Northwest

Seaborne Charters, Ltd.
Box 282
West Vancouver, B.C.

$380 a week for a Columbia 26.

San Juan Charters
Box 606
Friday Harbor, WA 98250

Boats from 24 to 40 feet.

Anacortes Yacht Charters
3005 Commercial Avenue
Anacortes, WA 98221

Over 50 boats; a Columbia 29 goes for $475, a husky Baba 30 for $645.

Great Lakes

Georgian Bay Yacht
Charter Co.
Box 152
Midland, Ontario

$515 for a C&C 31 (dropping to $365 July, August)

Sailboat Charter Service
980 W. Broadway
Muskegon, MI 49441

Irwin 30 or O'Day 32 for $600

Northeast

Hinckley Yacht Brokerage
Box 155
Southwest Harbor, ME
04679

30 boats, (30' to 50') from $600 to $2,000.

Windward Blue Sailing
1488 Washington
Cape May, NJ 08204

Pearson 35 for $600

Chesapeake

Hermes Marina   25′ to 45′ for from
4 Beach Rd. $225 to $750.
Sherwood Forest, MD
21405

Florida

Fun in the Sun   Learn-to-sail and learn-
1668 SE 17th St.   to-cruise programs:
Ft. Lauderdale, FL 33316   Irwin 37 for $900 ($800
                                 off-season, July to November).

Islands in the Sun   Learn-to-sail and learn-
1400 SE 17th St.   to-cruise programs;
Ft. Lauderdale, FL 33316   Irwin 37 for $850 ($700
                                 off-season).

Hirsh   Has learn-to-sail and
3 Marina Playa   learn-to-cruise programs;
Sarasota, FL 33577   Morgan 32 for $825; has
                                 "rent-it-here, leave-it-
                                 there" capability.

St. Petersburg Yacht   Wide variety of boats;
Charters   a Morgan 25 goes for $347,
400 Second Ave. NE   a Morgan 32 for $575 (12 per-
St. Petersburg, FL 33701   cent discount off-season).

Gulf of Mexico

CSY, Ltd.   Chartering in the Bay
P.O. Box 491   Islands of Honduras;
Tenafly, NJ 07670   a CSY 37 costs $1190
                                 ($952 or $714 during
                                 off-season periods).

Fleet Indigo   Operating out of Belize;
Box 9243   a Wings 33 for $1000 ($800
Treasure Island, FL 33740   or $600 off-season periods).

Bahamas

(Note: Cruising in the Bahamas has been risky of late, due to drug
 smugglers pirating sailboats and killing their crews.)

Abaco Bahamas Charter   A Morgan 28 goes for $900
10905 Cowgill Place   per week, dropping to $700
Middletown, KY 40243   for two weeks from July to
                                 November.

Bahamas Yachting Services   Learn-to-sail and learn-to-cruise
P.O. Box 21830   program; an Endeavor 32 for
Ft. Lauderdale, FL 33335 $850.

42

U.S. Virgin Islands

Avery's Boathouse
P.O. Box 3693
St. Thomas, USVI 00801

A Pearson 28 goes for $630, or $525 from May to December.

Caribbean Yacht Charter
P.O. Box 583
Marblehead, MA 01945

Morgan Out-Island 33 charters for $995—$650 or $750 off-season; learning programs.

Seabreeze Yacht Charter
550 Pharr Rd., Suite 822
Atlanta, GA 30305

Learn-to-sail and learn-to-cruise; Pearson 365 goes for $1,295, dropping to $645—795 off-season.

43

Sailaway, Inc.
P.O. Box 880
Hightstown, NJ 08520

Learn-to-sail and cruise programs; C&C 36 costs $1,295, but $645-795 off-season.

British Virgin Islands

Tortola Yacht Charters
21 Hale Lane
Darien, CT 06820

Learn-to-sail, learn-to-cruise; the C&C 36 goes for $1,370, or $820 to $1,030 off-season.

North South Yacht Charters
801 South Rancho Dr.,
Bld. B-1B
Las Vegas, NV 89106

Learn-to-sail and cruise programs; an Aloha 34 or Hughes 38 runs $1,155, or $910 off-season.

West Indies Yacht Charters
2190 SE 17th St.
Ft. Lauderdale, FL 33316

Learn-to-sail and cruise; a Cal 31 can be chartered in the off-season for $695 for 9 days.

Tropic Island
1712 Charles St.
Whitby, Ontario L1N 1C2

A Morgan Out-Island 41 goes for $1,295, but this drops to $735-975 off-season.

West Indies (Lesser Antilles)

(Note: Chartering in the Lesser Antilles, or the Leeward and Windward Islands as they are known to yachtsmen, tends to be expensive. The following represent the only large companies at anything close to reasonable rates.)

The Moorings
P.O. Box 50059
New Orleans, LA 70150

Sailing from St. Lucia; a big Mariner 39 for $2,570 for 10 days, which drops to $1,450 from August through November.

Leeward Islands Yacht
Charters
43 N. Pleasant Ave.
Ridgewood, NJ 07450

Operates out of St. Maarten; learn-to-sail and learn-to-cruise programs; Pearson 390 for $1,330, or $798-931 off-season.

Spice Island Charters P.O. Box 1183, Station Q Toronto, Ontario M4T 2P4	From Grenada; learn-to-sail and learn-to-cruise: a C&C 36 for $1,330, or $875-1,100 off-season.

Greece

United Yacht Charters 1420 S. 9th Alhambra, CA 91803	25- to 200-foot boats, from $420 to $14,000 a week.
Greek Private Sailing Club 600 B St. Andrews Rd. Philadelphia, PA 19118	Jaguar 25s & 27s for $490-$700.
Island Sailing, Ltd. Northney Marina, Hayling Island Hampshire, England	Depending on season, between 672 and 1288 pounds sterling for a couple aboard a Dufour 28, for two weeks.

South Pacific

South Pacific Yacht Charter P.O. Box 6 Smithfield, UT 84335	Operating out of Kingdom of Tonga; their Nautical 39 goes for $1,400.

(Note: This new operation offers sailing in the Vaváu and Há apai island groups; a bit expensive—though not for size of boat—but the only outfit to offer a valuable exposure to South Pacific cruising.)

By way of price comparison, a scanning of the private owner classified ads in mid-1981 showed, for example, a Tartan 34 in Florida for $550 a week; a Morgan Out-Island 41 in the Bahamas for $800 a week; a Catalina 30 in Washington's San Juans for $455 a week; and a Rhodes Seafarer 38 in the Chesapeake for $500 a week.

Give chartering a try if you have questions in your mind about how you or your family will take to cruising. Chartering a boat can be pretty expensive, but it is a heck of a lot cheaper than discovering you are not cut out for the cruising life after you have already uprooted your family, sold the house for a boat, and are halfway to Hawaii!

Part 2
Some Economic Facts

5

The Costs of Cruising

Most of the luxuries, and many of the so-called comforts, of life are not only not indispensable, but positive hindrances to the elevation of mankind.

In the "old days," it was possible to build a wooden boat in your backyard for maybe a couple of hundred dollars and then take off around the world with a few silver coins in your pocket. Joshua Slocum did it. So did Dumas, and Moitessier, and a number of other rugged old salts. But those days, unfortunately, are gone.

Today, a seaworthy sailboat can easily run over $100,000 if you go first-cabin, and the operating costs can quickly wipe out whatever savings you have managed to scrape together. But it needn't. Let's talk costs.

What does it cost to cruise today? Well, the potential cruiser is looking at two expenses—one fixed, one running. His fixed initial expense is the price of his cruising vessel; once paid for, that expense ceases, and the boat represents a saleable asset. His running expenses are the costs of such items as food, supplies, maintenance, taxes, and fees; these will vary somewhat but will be continuous.

Let's take a look at these two expenses.

Boats are obviously more expensive in today's market—everything is. On the other hand, the better boats of today are superior in design and materials—if not always craftsmanship—to those of yesterday. But that fact does not help your pocketbook when it comes to buying the boat. Face it: That brand-new beauty of a 36-foot ketch with fiberglass hull, aluminum masts, roller reefing, electronic auto pilot, and radar has a price tag of $90,000.

Buying a boat is much like buying a car. We would all like to get a Mercedes, a Porsche, or maybe a sexy Lamborghini. It would set us back $40,000 or so, but we would have a real machine, a speedster that would drive like a dream and outperform most everything on the road. But we do not have $40,000. So we look in the Volvo and BMW dealer's showrooms. Very nice cars, but the tag is still over fifteen grand. What is it we want? And what can we get it for? Well, basically we want a set of wheels that will take us from place to place in relative safety, comfort, and economy. Then why not look in the used car classifieds? There are three-year-old Chevies and VWs in there for two or three thousand. Granted that there will be some dents in the fender and the ashtrays may need emptying, but the machine will still fill our needs—and for a fraction of the price of newer, more sophisticated vehicles.

The same with boats. A beautiful new Valiant 40 is going to carry a tag of over a hundred grand. Fine, if you can afford it. The Valiant is one of the best cruising boats currently sailing the seas. But if you could afford it, you would probably not be reading this book. Coming down a peg from a Valiant 40, we find that we can sail away in a new Ericson 35 for about fifty grand. Another good boat, the Ericson— maybe not quite the quality or size of the Valiant, but a good sailer. Yet fifty grand is just beyond our pocketbook.

What is it we want? A strong, seakindly sailboat that we can live aboard comfortably and that will carry us through the changeable conditions of the seas in relative safety and with some speed. Well, what is wrong with buying a used boat? Used sailboats do not depreciate in value as rapidly as cars do; in fact, some popular models will actually appreciate—particularly if they are loaded down with expensive equipment. Generally, however, used boats will be less expensive than the newer versions. A Westsail 32, for example, which sold new for $70,000 may be going five years later for $55,000. Yet a thorough survey of the vessel may show absolutely nothing wrong; the boat is in perfect running condition.

There are benefits to buying a boat used that have no counterpart in buying a car. First, most new boats are going to have initial problems; a used boat will have had most of these "kinks" ironed out. Second, the used boat—particularly if it is a cruiser—will probably come with a considerable amount of equipment. That Westsail 32 came from the factory bare; it is now on the market used but with a depth finder, transmitter-receiver, self-steering vane, dinghy, life raft, anchors and line, spare sails, and so on. That $55,000 used Westsail would have cost $85,000 new—not $70,000—if it had been thus equipped.

Rule 1: *Buy used*.

Your second consideration in the cost of a boat is the size. Do you really need a 36-footer? Have you been aboard some of the better-designed 28- or 30-foot jobs? The cost of a boat increases exponentially—not arithmetically—with its size. Where a 30-foot sloop will cost, say, $25,000, that same manufacturer's 34-foot version may run $35,000 or more. Of course, if you have a big family, you need a larger boat. But in shopping for your new home at sea, try to understand that this is a whole new lifestyle: You simply will not need the room you think you do. Space equals money and work in a boat. A larger boat costs more initially; it costs more to maintain; the slip fees and harbor duties will be higher; and there will be more work for you to keep it in shape.

Before you make any hasty decisions, take a look at Pacific Seacraft's Flicka 20. At 20 feet, this pocket world cruiser has an incredible amount of room; in fact, her designer and his wife have lived happily aboard their own Flicka for the past three years. Now, you will probably find this too small for your own needs, but ask yourself: If a sturdy, seaworthy 20-foot boat can provide a safe and comfortable home to a naval architect and his wife, do *you* really need 36 feet? Then take a look at some 30-footers and reassess your needs. As with the used Chevy or VW, ask yourself what you *need*.

Rule 2: *Think Small*

Now, 95 percent of the sailboats rolling off the assembly lines have fiberglass hulls and fiberglass or teak decks. And glass is nice; it is light, strong, does not rot or rust, and requires little maintenance. It is also expensive.

If you can afford a good used fiberglass boat, get it. Purists and tradition aside, glass hulls have proven themselves over and over. Given a choice between glass and any other material, you should probably choose glass. And the majority of used boats you will be looking at will have glass hulls.

But consider wood: It is easy to work on, it offers good insulation, and repair materials are easy to come by. It is also cheap. There is nothing intrinsically wrong with a wooden sailboat. They can be as fast, safe, and comfortable as a fiberglass boat; world cruises are

50

Pacific Seacraft's Flicka—at 20 feet, the smallest seaworthy world cruiser made.

commonly made in wood boats, and races are won with them. Yet the prices on used wood boats are drastically lower than for comparable glass boats. Why? Demand. The yachting public wants only the best, the latest, the most advanced in design and materials; wood is, well, old-fashioned. It is not in vogue. And so it goes begging.

There is no reason why you should not take a long look at used wood boats on the market today. A well-designed 30-foot fiberglass sloop may cost $25,000 used; the same basic design in wood may only run $15,000. Of course, some wood boats will be poor buys—the wood rotten or the design simply inefficient. But many will be good, solid sailers, ready and able to take on a world-circling cruise. You will have more work to do on the boat during the cruise. But won't you have plenty of time?

Rule 3: *Don't ignore wood.*

We will leave until a later chapter the discussion of specific sailboats suitable for cruising and their price tags. For now, you should realize that there is a tremendous range in prices when looking for a cruiser. An old, time-proven 25-foot wooden Folkboat capable of sailing the world safely can be had today for $6,000. You can go the whole route and spend well over a hundred grand for a new Hans Christian 43. Or you can find something in between—a good, solid used 32-footer for $25,000. Any of them will get you where you want to go. It is up to you whether you want to arrive in a shiny Rolls Royce or a slightly tarnished VW.

Don't forget to add the costs of equipment to the boat you finally buy. No matter how well equipped, there are probably going to be a few items you are going to want to add. And that can cost $500 or $10,000, depending on you and your needs.

So much for the initial expense of buying the boat. Let's now consider the running expenses of cruising.

Again, the old days are gone. You can no longer just drop anchor in Tahiti and live off coconuts and taro forever. Today, the bureaucrats and merchants have taken over in most places. Red tape aside, there are going to be a lot of hands in your pockets when you arrive in some countries. There are customs duties, harbor taxes, anchorage fees; you may have to show proof of solvency. Food and supplies continue to become more expensive each inflationary year, and the boys in white robes have sent fuel prices into the heavens.

Yet it can be done. You, your wife, and two children can cruise comfortably on $300 a month. If you are single, that figure will be $200 a month.

It takes little effort to run that figure up to a thousand bucks a month. All you have to do is what so many yacht owners do. First off, when you arrive in a new port you lay up alongside a dock or yacht club and pay an exorbitant slip fee. Then you go ashore, and do your dining at the local restaurants. Buy plenty of things wherever you go—particularly tourist goods. When you go shopping for provisions, buy nothing but imported American food and canned goods; in other words, maintain the same basic diet you had in the States. Make sure you have plenty of expensive thingamajigs aboard to go on the blink, such as electrical refrigeration, power windlasses, and a pressurized hot-water system. Hire local tradesmen or sailors on nearby boats to do all of the repairs and maintenance work aboard your yacht. And, oh yes, run that big auxiliary engine as often as possible.

Of course, there is another way. And that way is to adapt to the environment and to be as self-sufficient as possible.

When you arrive in a new place, drop anchor rather than pay dockage; anchoring is usually free, and the short dinghy ride is good for you, right? Eating at restaurants is a luxury, particularly when your boat is fully stocked and your cook is adept in the galley. When you reprovision, buy the local goods—bananas, papaya, pig, chickens, whatever. There are very few places you will be sailing to where your nutritional needs cannot be met by adapting to local eating habits.

Another thing: Keep the boat's equipment simple. When something goes wrong, fix it yourself, or at least try to; you will be surprised how knowledgeable even the least mechanically inclined sailor can become when he has to. And as for the engine, expensive fuel should only be burned when necessary—and once you become experienced at sailing to and off anchor, it will rarely be necessary.

Clothing can be made from fabric, and old clothing patched up. Food can be heavily supplemented with fish from the sea and perhaps even fruit and vegetables gathered ashore. Invitations to dinner from natives or fellow cruisers are common, though these should be reciprocated. Supplies and services can often be obtained through bartering. Taking along a supply of such items as blue jeans on your cruise is a wise idea; they are prized—and expensive—in most corners of the world. Collect useful items during your voyage for possible trade; what is junk on one island may be valuable on another.

In other words, be as materially self-sufficient as possible and adapt to the local conditions and people. Accomplish these dual goals, and you will do more than just save a pile of money. First, you will gain independence—financially, materially, spiritually. There is a terrific feeling that comes from knowing that you can take care of yourself and your family, that you are a self-contained unit that needs nothing materially that you cannot supply. Not to mention that you will be much safer at sea knowing how to deal with problems yourself when no one else is available. Second, you will have a hell of a better time with the citizens of the countries you visit if you accept their ways, eat their food, blend with them.

Think about it.

So what will it cost? Well, figure for a family of four—skipper, wife, two little deckhands—that there will be expenses of about $170 a month for food, $10 for fuel, $20 for the bureaucrats, $50 for maintenance and repair, and $50 for supplies (soap, charts, etc.). That is $300 a month. Of course, there will be months when that figure will go considerably higher (the engine may suddenly quit, requiring a $250 part to put it right). But there will also be months when the running expenses approach zero. If you are going to cruise the Mediterranean, costs will go up; cruise the South Pacific (outside of Tahiti), costs will go down.

Freedom and adventure. On $300 a month. Not bad.

As an item of interest, consider the following comparison of costs aboard a paid-off boat with living in a house or apartment for a husband, wife, and two kids.

	House	Boat
Rent/mortgage	$500	0
Food	420	170
Automobile (payment, fuel, insurance)	350	10
Utilities (incl. phone)	120	0
Insurance (house, life)	80	0
Maintenance/repairs	75	50
Entertainment	100	0
Taxes (property taxes, entry fees, other taxes)	80	20
Supplies (laundry, charts, etc.)	75	40
Miscellaneous (including medical, furnishings, clothing)	200	10
	$1,900	$300

Still think you can't afford to go cruising?

6

The 1-Year Plan

*If one advances confidently in the direction of his dreams, and
endeavors to live the life which he has imagined, he will meet with a
success unexpected in common hours.*

And now for the heart of this book—a simple plan enabling you to
retire aboard your own sailboat within one year, free to find a new
lifestyle cruising the oceans of the world.

There is, of course, nothing magical about the plan. As with most
realistic long-term projects, it is based upon equal parts of common
sense and discipline. It does not presume that the reader earns a large
salary or already has a huge bank account. On the contrary, the plan
assumes that the reader makes an average salary at an average job and
has absolutely nothing in the bank to begin with. If money is available,
so much the better—the 1-year plan becomes a 6-month plan. Nor does
this plan proceed on the theory that the reader has only himself to
consider. Again, the presumption will be made here that the reader has
the responsibility of a wife and two young children. As will be seen,
however, this family can be turned from a financial liability into an
asset in working for the common goal of a better life afloat.

All right, let's take a look at our model family, which wants to
find the freedom of the seas but feels helpless in the face of financial
"reality." John Peters is thirty-five years old, employed by his

community as a policeman. He earns about $19,000 a year and takes
home about $16,000 of that after taxes; he is a long way from a
pension, his retirement not coming for another fifteen years. He owns
a home worth about $60,000, with an equity of about $10,000; his
monthly mortgage payments, including insurance and property taxes,
run $400 per month. The Peters family has two cars—an old Ford
station wagon and a three-year-old Chevy Blazer. The two cars are
worth a total of about $8,000, of which only $4,000 represents equity;
the payments on one car loan amounts to $150 a month. The only
other assets John has worth noting are a life-insurance policy, on
which he pays $75 per month, and assorted household furniture. He
has absolutely no money in the bank, owns no stocks or bonds, and
has invested in no real estate other than his own home.

55

John's wife, Sally, was a secretary when she first met her
husband. She is now a full-time housewife, occupied with trying to
balance a precarious budget, maintain a home, and raise their two
children—ages eight and ten. Like most families, Sally finds it
increasingly difficult to "make ends meet" in an inflationary economy;
each year, John's paycheck seems to grow less than the prices at the
supermarket, and clothing their two boys requires ever-more-careful
shopping at discount stores.

In short, John Peters is like millions of other Americans today—
nearly broke but for a small equity in his house, living precariously
from payday to payday. How, then, can he even *dream* of retiring to a
life of cruising the oceans of the world aboard his own sailboat? He
must, after all, be realistic: Boats are expensive. Where is he going to
get $30,000 or $40,000 for a blue-water cruiser? He does not begin to
have enough to buy it for cash. Obviously, he doesn't have anything
left over from his paycheck to put aside toward the boat price; even if
he could manage to squirrel away $100 a month, it would take him
thirty years to save up enough for such a boat. And he cannot buy it on
credit: He couldn't afford the monthly payments, particularly at
today's interest rates. In any event, no bank would consider him
qualified for such a loan after looking at his income/expenses ledger.

So John can't buy a boat, can't get a loan, and can't even save up
for one. On top of that, he is going to need thousands of dollars of
equipment for extended deep-water cruising. And what about
maintenance and repairs? And have we forgotten that he has to feed,
clothe, and care for his wife and children while afloat? Just where is he
going to make a living as a policeman in the middle of the ocean? No,
to take off on a boat requires another ten or twenty grand at the very
least, safely tucked away in a bank. Clearly, it is financially impossible
for John Peters to realize his dream.

Or is it? *Within one year*, John and his family can be setting sail for Tahiti aboard their own sailboat—a seaworthy vessel bought and paid for. They can have a bank account of $20,000 from which to make occasional withdrawals for living expenses, and they will have no loans or other financial obligations sucking away at them. They can be free—free of the drudgery of land life, free of enslaving financial needs, free to explore the world and regain health through experiencing nature.

This is not an idle dream, not a half-baked scheme to "get rich quick." It is simply the application of common sense, and requires only one thing—*dedication*. In other words, John Peters and his family can achieve their goal if they *want* it badly enough. They can achieve it by following a simple plan, a plan which requires a great deal of *self-discipline*. And if John Peters can find his new life within one year, you, the reader, certainly can. John has little in the way of assets, no savings, an income that is barely enough to meet expenses, a nonworking wife, and the responsibility of two young children. In all probability, you are in considerably better shape financially than John. Perhaps you have investments, perhaps you are a foot-loose bachelor, perhaps you have a large equity in your home, or perhaps you have a retirement pension. All to the better, of course—it will enable you to take significant short-cuts to the goal of finding a better life afloat. The point is simple: If John Peters can do it by following the 1-Year Plan, then almost anyone can.

So what is this fantastic "1-Year Plan"? The plan is quite simple, really, consisting of five logical steps outlined as follows:

1. *Liquidate assets*
2. *Purchase boat*
3. *Expand employment*
4. *Budget strictly*
5. *Save*

As a result of following this plan carefully, John Peters can expect to have a paid-off sailboat at the end of one year, to have accumulated the necessary equipment for a world cruise, and to have a kitty in the neighborhood of $20,000. And all it takes is *discipline*.

Let's take a look at this plan.

1. **Liquidate assets.** The first thing John Peters must do is ruthlessly wipe out his "estate." He must sell the house, sell the furniture, sell the two cars. Nor does it end there. Through holding garage sales and placing advertisements in the local newspapers, he must sell almost everything else he and his family own—television,

stereo, microwave oven, clothes washer and dryer, kitchen utensils, books, clothing, etc. He must keep only two things in mind while he is purging his accumulated possessions of many years: What will we be taking with us on board the boat? What will we need during the year before we actually leave on our voyage?

It is really remarkable, once the liquidation phase begins, to see how many possessions most of us have. We are a consumer society, an object-oriented culture, and this is reflected in the incredible quantity and variety of gizmos and doohickies we own. Without fully realizing it, most of us have acquired a vast array of things and devices, most of which are not necessary but designed only as luxuries. Is a television really *needed*? Does listening to music require a thousand dollars' worth of stereo components? Can't we cook without a microwave and a Cuisinart? Are the books we own available at the local library? Do we really need five suits, four sport coats, and six pairs of dress shoes?

The irony of John's purge of his possessions is likely to be that he begins to experience not a sense of loss at seeing all of his material goods being sold off but rather a sense of *elation*. For it is a very real fact of life that our possessions increasingly tend to possess *us*. And as they begin to disappear, a strange feeling of relief begins to spread—a sensation not unlike that of someone who is regaining his freedom. Of course, many people, perhaps *most* people, would never feel this sensation; they would feel only a sense of loss, if not a terrifying panic. But, then, most people would not find the freedom and adventure of the cruising life a comfortable feeling either. If you are the type of person who seeks that life, who feels suffocated by the traditional values and lifestyles of our cities today, then you are probably also the kind of individual who will feel relief from ridding yourself of the endless trappings of that lifestyle. Not, of course, that you will not experience some initial doubts and nervousness at systematically eliminating most of what you own. You are, after all, a product of this society, and you have been constantly reminded that your life is measured in terms of possessions.

All right. John has sold the house and paid off the mortgage, pocketing $10,000 in equity. And he has managed to sell both cars, paying off the one car loan and clearing another $4,000. The furniture, television, washer and dryer, and stereo equipment brought $4,000 more. And placing a number of classified ads, and holding a couple of garage sales, resulted in the liquidation of kitchen utensils, china and crystal, bicycles, record albums, books, clothing—all to the tune of $2,400 more. Grand total: $20,400.

But there is more. John has to cash in his life-insurance policy. (We will ignore the possibilities of cashing in his retirement benefits— which may result in a sizeable sum). And here is perhaps where we really come to grips with the change in lifestyles. For society has convinced most of us that a man is totally selfish if he does not plan for the well being of his family in the event of his death. In this materialistic culture, a man is viewed in terms of what he can materially produce, a family in terms of what it materially needs. In other words, a man represents nothing more than a potential *estate*. He is bombarded from an early age with the concept that he must prepare for his death by creating possessions to care for his wife and children. Never mind that the wife can probably earn a decent salary nowadays; never mind that the children will have been self-sufficient and with families of their own long before the father dies; never mind that if the one-in-a-thousand occurs and the husband dies at an early age, the wife will usually remarry. And never mind that the *present* quality of life suffers because of this preoccupation with preparing for death.

What is insurance to you? It is a gamble, a crap-shoot—and you, the shooter, are simply taking the odds against yourself. The insurance companies—which have become disgustingly wealthy by inundating us with a belief in the need for their questionable services—would have you believe that by taking out life-insurance policies you are bettering the lives of your loved ones. Horse pucky! Betting on your own death is a *denial* of life; love is expressed by giving of yourself *now*—not after you are dead.

Well, you are going to have one of two reactions to cashing in any life-insurance policies. Either you are going to feel the same sense of relief—albeit a nervous relief at first—as when you unloaded your house and goods, or you are going to be miserable, unable to venture into the future without the security of "a piece of the rock" behind you. If you are the former, then the cruising way of life was meant for you. But if you are the latter type, then you would be much better off recognizing at this early stage that the voyaging lifestyle is not for you; the uncertainties of real freedom, and the sole dependence upon your own knowledge and skills, will simply cause you anxiety and unhappiness. So perhaps this is a good point at which to assess your values . . . and possibly avoid committing yourself further to a futile effort.

Consider, now, John's changing financial status. With $4,700 obtained from the life-insurance policy, he now has $25,100 in the bank. But consider also what he has *eliminated*. John no longer has a mortgage payment to make on the house; the local property taxes and house insurance have also been eliminated, along with utility bills. He will no longer be making monthly a payment on the automobile; car insurance for both cars has also been done away with, along with gasoline, maintenance, and repair costs. And the life-insurance

58

premiums have been eliminated. In other words, the monthly expenses have been drastically reduced. And he has only just begun.

Fine, you say, but the Peters family is also without a home or car!

As a part of this first phase of the 1-Year Plan, John must buy a reliable but inexpensive used car—one which will get him to and from work, will require minimal gas and maintenance, and will have a probable resale value in a year of about what he paid for it: a used Volkswagen beetle, for example, or an old clunker of a Chevy. It isn't pretty, it won't impress the neighbors—but it will do the job economically. The minimal legally required car insurance should be carried. Of course, if using public transportation is possible, no car is necessary.

So much for the Peters' family car. As for their future home . . . that brings up the second phase of the plan.

2. **Purchase boat.** The second step is sheer joy—shopping for, and buying, the vessel that will be home for the future. It will, of course, be more than a home; it will be a passport to adventure, a ticket to freedom, the direct means of achieving a more rewarding life.

The actual details of shopping for the right boat, inspecting it, financing, etc., will be left for later chapters. For now, suffice it to answer the obvious questions: Why buy the boat right now? And how can I afford to buy it?

The boat should be bought as early in the 1-Year Plan as possible, bearing in mind the limitations of your knowledge about what you need and want in a boat. You should be looking over the boat market immediately and buying one as soon as you are confident of what you are looking for. That is not to say that you should run right out and buy a boat—any acceptable boat. The vessel will be more than home in the years to come, and your judgment in its selection will be directly reflected in safety, comfort, and pride of ownership. The selection of such a boat is infinitely more important than the choice of a house. Rather, step two of the plan envisions the purchase of a boat at the earliest *practical* opportunity—that is, as soon as you know what you are looking for.

Why? For a number of very good reasons. First, the family will have a home in which to live during the one-year period. The house has been sold, and the family needs a place to live. Why not live aboard *now* rather than wait for a year? Why pay rent for an apartment, when you can live aboard your own boat for about the same amount in monthly payments on the boat mortgage? In fact, the boat payments may very well be less than prevailing rents in the area and probably less also than the mortgage payments were on the house. Rent,

59

however, is money gone; payments on the boat are an investment in the future of the plan, each payment a step toward the cruising life. And, of course, the interest on the boat payments is tax deductible.

So it makes financial sense: While in the process of buying the boat, it provides you with a home at no additional cost. Or, to put it another way, you are buying the boat with the rent money.

A second very good reason for buying the boat at the outset is also financial in nature. We are living in times of constant inflation. What today costs a dollar may well cost a dollar and twenty cents in a year. This is particularly true of sailboats. The materials that go into a good boat—fiberglass hull, teak decks, mahogany interior, copper tubing, stainless steel tanks, brass fittings—are becoming more and more difficult to obtain. Thus, a well-designed and-constructed sailboat that costs $30,000 today may end up costing you $35,000 at the end of your 1-Year Plan. And this is obviously self-defeating: You are merely running in place if the one-year wait ends up costing you hard-earned savings in inflated boat prices.

If the boat is purchased at the beginning of the plan, however, the owner experiences the benefits—rather than the costs—of inflation. Quite simply, he owns an appreciating asset. Assuming the boat is well cared for (and there is nothing like living aboard to guarantee that), it should increase in value as time goes by. This will probably more than compensate for the interest paid on the boat mortgage during the one-year period.

If you need any further reasons for buying the boat right away, there are many. Consider, for example, that before you take off on the first leg of your new life at sea, you must properly equip the boat, purchase and store supplies, "sea trial" the boat, iron out all the kinks, and completely familiarize yourself with every nook and cranny of the vessel. This can take many weeks, if not months, under the best of circumstances. By buying the boat first, though, these chores can be accomplished with considerably more ease and thoroughness during the year preceding departure.

Yet another benefit is that living aboard provides an opportunity both to begin acclimating to the new lifestyle and to find out if it is really what you are looking for. Rather than jumping from a house or apartment onto a boat a few days before sailing off for good, living aboard from the beginning permits the family to adapt more slowly to this new way of life while still maintaining their contact with land; the transition will prove more gradual, less of a shock. At the same time, this taste of what life will be like may offer the opportunity to assess your needs and desires honestly. All romance aside, living in a confined space under Spartan conditions is not for everyone (thank

God!). And there is no better way to find out than by actually undergoing the live-aboard experience in the safety of a dockside environment. Finding out now that it is just not the ticket can save a lot of grief later on—after you have quit your job and burned your bridges.

If even further reason is needed for buying that boat early in the plan, consider the savings in entertainment costs for the family. Of course, John Peters, his wife, and children will be on a severe budget during their 1-Year Plan, but there must be some outlet—some form of recreation and entertainment—or morale and family unity will be severely strained. What better form of recreation than sailing? The new home is also the new source of entertainment! For most people, yachting is an expensive form of recreation; for the Peters family, it doesn't cost a nickel.

So much for the *why* of buying the boat at the beginning. Now, as to the *how* . . .

Again, let's take John Peters' situation. His financial picture has drastically improved. He now has $25,100 in the bank, with no debts, and his monthly expenses have been reduced dramatically. Suddenly, his take-home salary represents about double his monthly expenditures. In other words, he now represents an entirely different picture to a bank looking at him as a loan prospect.

Let's assume John has found the boat of his dreams, and the price tag is $30,000. Now, basically, he can approach the purchase in different ways. The traditional way is to place the required 20 percent down and finance the remainder with a bank or other lending institution. The loan would then be paid at the end of the one-year period—either prematurely, or according to schedule, depending upon how the repayment was set up. A second way is to make a down payment of as much as possible—say, $20,000 of the $25,100 in assets John now has—and finance only the remaining $10,000 for a year. Yet a third possibility, if available, is to negotiate a private contract with the boat's owner, asking him to take back "paper" on any unpaid balance.

The first method is the least desirable. The interest being earned on John's assets may be anywhere from 5 percent in a bank to 13 percent or so in something like a money account or bonds. The interest he is paying on the loan, however, will be closer to 15 percent. Therefore, he should place as much of his liquid assets as payment on the boat as possible, saving enough to begin repairing and equipping the boat. Whether dealing with a bank or with a private party, then, John should place $20,000 down on the boat and arrange for financing on the $10,000 balance (care should be taken, of course, to preclude any prepayment-penalty clauses should the agreement involve a loan period of more than one year).

John has not only presented a healthier picture of his personal finances to the lender, he has also placed two-thirds of the total purchase price down on the boat—or about three times more than is usually required by lending institutions. The bank or lender could not feel more protected: The value of the boat/collateral is three times the amount of the loan. In other words, John has suddenly become an attractive credit risk.

3. **Expand employment**. Now we return to the more unpleasant realities of the 1-Year Plan—realities that will require dedication and self-sacrifice.

John Peters is a police officer, working a forty-hour week. Quite simply, he will have to get a second, part-time job, working another ten or twenty hours every week. With John, private security work is a natural, and the hours can usually be made to fit his regular work schedule. There are, of course, hundreds of other possibilities— bartending, construction work, driving a cab, sales, etc. The important thing to remember here is that neither pride nor status nor working conditions has any place in the 1-Year Plan; the *only* consideration is putting together enough money to start a new life in one year. If you have to dig ditches or sell vacuum cleaners door-to-door, so be it. And if a part-time management trainee earns $125 a week while a part-time garbage collector earns $150, you start slinging garbage.

But it doesn't all fall on John's shoulders. Sally now finds herself liberated from most of the chores that tied her to the house; living aboard has given her time on her hands. There is absolutely no reason why she should not go out and get a full-time job. The children are at school during the day, and she is fortunate enough to have a marketable skill, once she polishes her typing up a bit. Again, however, whatever her skills, she will take the job that pays the most money. Status, working conditions, opportunities for advancement, retirement programs and other fringe benefits—all of these are secondary to the size of the paychecks for the next year.

One of the beautiful things about the 1-Year Plan is how quickly it brings families together. Where a family once loaded down with all the benefits of a material society constantly fought with one another, that family now living an austere existence is pulling together as one in their mutual pursuit of a shining goal.

John's two kids are eight and ten years of age and, like most kids would be, excited about this new adventure. What child would not be thrilled at the prospect of sailing the seas, the world his classroom? In all probability, John's boys will want to pitch in—and they should. They can help keep the boat well-maintained, but they too are fully capable of getting jobs—if nothing more than delivering papers before school or mowing lawns after. Every little bit of income helps; over a one-year period, the income from the boys' paper routes alone might buy a badly needed set of sails or an overhaul of the boat's engine. More importantly, perhaps, the children will have felt—rightfully— that they have sacrificed and contributed toward achieving the mutual dream.

End result? In addition to his income of $19,000 as a police officer, John is now drawing another $7,000 from his part-time job as a security guard. Sally has landed a position with a law firm as a full-time secretary, earning $11,000 a year. And the two boys are working paper routes and mowing lawns, clearing around $50 a month each. Projected over the coming year, this represents about $19,000 over and above John's salary as an officer—or about $38,000 in all.

4. **Budget strictly**. Let's assume that the Peters family bought their dream boat for $30,000, paying $20,000 down and financing the rest over a period of five years (they plan to pay it off prematurely after one year). This leaves them with $5,100 remaining of the cash realized from liquidating their home, cars, and most of their personal possessions. Their projected total gross income for the coming year is $38,000, of which about $33,000 will be cleared after taxes. Adding the $5,100, the Peterses can expect to have about $38,000 over the next year. But from that amount, they must make the monthly boat payment, add any equipment necessary for the voyage, begin storing supplies, pay slip fees and marine insurance (required by the lender), maintain and repair the boat—as well as the normal expenses of food, gas, clothing, and so on.

Obviously, a strict budget must be drawn up and adhered to. Every dollar not spent during the year is a dollar that will stretch three times farther at sea.

The family car should be a relatively minor cost; it should be purchased used with the intention of selling it a year later for about the same price. If a car can be done away with altogether, relying upon public transportation, fine! The costs of gasoline, oil, repairs, and auto insurance are thereby avoided.

Food should prove less expensive than previously, once the family adjusts to eating basic, wholesome meals and gives up TV dinners, steaks, and fancy foods. Reducing or cutting out alcoholic beverages and cigarettes can not only be a healthy step but an economical one (it is amazing how many beneficial side effects there are to spending less money).

Clothing is no longer a source of great expense. In all probability, the family can exist quite well for a year with the clothing they already have; only so many clothes will fit into a boat, in any event. Style will no longer be a consideration; utility and comfort are paramount. As a result, clothing will cost less—and can even be made aboard the boat, if someone has the ability (or learns it).

Rent is gone, replaced by a smaller boat-loan payment. Assuming the boat is kept at a marina, the utilities—water, electricity—will usually be paid by the operators of the marina. As to a telephone (assuming that telephone service is available to a boat), is it really necessary? Again, the budget is a severe one, and what has been considered a necessity in the past may now be a luxury.

Of course, there will be expenses that are probably unavoidable: slip fees, marine insurance, maintenance and repair. The insurance will be required by the lender; once the boat is paid for, marine insurance is best left behind along with life insurance, car insurance, health insurance, house insurance, unemployment insurance—and all the other ploys of the big corporations which bury us in security.

Slip fees are probably unavoidable. Certainly, life dockside at a marina is much more pleasant than being anchored in the middle of a harbor or tied alongside a river wall. The availability of utility hook-ups, easy access by foot, the presence of toilets and showers ashore—all are nice. A really dedicated family can, however, eliminate even this expense by simply dropping anchor—assuming this is legally permissible in the area—and commuting by dinghy. This saves anywhere from $50 to $200 a month for a 30-foot boat.

These are only a few examples of ways in which living expenses can be drastically reduced. There are hundreds of others, applicable according to the circumstances. The important thing here is the spirit— the willingness to exercise control, the desire to sacrifice, to reach a better way of life.

5. **Save.** Finally, a brief—and perhaps unnecessary—word about saving. We are living in inflationary times, as can readily be seen. It has been frequently observed that the borrowers and spenders benefit in such times, and the savers suffer; the savings are all too quickly eroded in terms of real purchasing power. Yet the 1-Year Plan depends upon severely curtailed spending together with a crash savings program. How can the savings be protected?

It must be recognized that a certain degree of safety is required in the investment of savings. While stocks and other such investments may (or may not) keep pace or even outdistance inflation, they are simply too risky; even bonds, in an era of fluctuating interest rates, could prove a chancy venture. Playing the commodities market, of course, is a gamble, pure and simple. Attempting to invest in tangibles such as gold, silver, stamps, or antiques is equally a gamble; a sudden drop in the market could wipe out your dream of cruising for a while.

Yet the relative safety of a bank's savings account is obtained at a cost: The interest rate is considerably less than the prevailing rate of inflation. Watching your savings steadily shrink in terms of purchasing power is not a pleasant experience.

Probably the best solution to the savings/investment problem is to place the money in a money-fund account. There are many such accounts available to the public today, offering interest rates which fluctuate and reflect the prevailing market. Where a bank may pay 7 or 8 percent a certificate, for example, money funds may be returning 10 to 15 percent—with no real loss in security. Interest rates will fluctuate, but the relative amounts reflected here will remain valid. In addition, the bank certificates tie the funds up for a period of time—six months, a year; with the money fund, however, the depositor-investor can actually write checks (uaually only for a minimal amount, such as $500) on the account and can add to or close the account almost as quickly as with a bank—and with no premature withdrawal penalty.

The 1-Year Planner, then, is probably best advised to deposit his money as it is earned in a relatively liquid money-fund account. Thus, the interest earned should at least keep your savings abreast with inflation.

John Peters was making $19,000 a year, of which he cleared $16,000. Before embarking on the 1-Year Plan, his expenses amounted to $16,000 per year. The last line on the Peters family ledger, therefore, read *zero*. Now, with the 1-Year Plan in effect, the Peters family will clear—after taxes—about $33,000 over the next year. At the same time, total expenses will have dropped from $16,000 a year to about half of that—$8,000. At the end of the period, therefore, the Peters family will have saved approximately $25,000; with the $5,100 left after making the down payment on the boat, the total savings is $30,000. Assuming that $2,000 of the $10,000 boat mortgage has been paid off during the year, the remaining $8,000 is paid out of the $30,000.

The Peters family began with no income in excess of expenditures, no liquid assets, and only a small equity in their home and cars. After a year of pulling together for a very real dream, they now own outright a $30,000 boat that has probably appreciated to

$33,000. Out of the $22,000 left after paying off the boat mortgage, they purchased $2,000 worth of supplies—and have $20,000 left over to finance their new way of life (the interest on this money has managed to offset inflationary pressures for them). Assuming that the Peterses can keep their cruising costs down to $300 a month, that $20,000 should keep them afloat for about six years (and as will shortly be seen, this can be supplemented by part-time work while cruising, thus extending "retirement" indefinitely).

At the same time, the Peterses used this one-year earning period to familiarize themselves with the boat, to shake out the "bugs," to add any necessary equipment, and, most importantly, to adjust to living aboard and to find out if this new lifestyle was what they were looking for. The boat was used not only as a home during this one-year savings period but as a source of recreation and entertainment as well.

After one year, the money was ready. But so were the Peterses. They had worked together, preparing the boat and themselves for the new life. They had learned about blue-water cruising, navigation, diesel mechanics, rigging, oceanography, cooking aboard, etc. Everything dovetailed beautifully: The year gave them the money, but it also gave them the experience and knowledge—knowledge of the boat, the sea, and of themselves. And it brought them closer together as a family.

The Peters family is, of course, a fiction—although based upon fact. The important point is that it can be done. The figures will change according to individual circumstances and the times in which we live, but the principle will not: work, discipline, sacrifice. If anything, John Peters and his family were worse off financially than are 90 percent of the readers of this book. Certainly, the plan can be shortened considerably if the reader is a bachelor or if he or she is retired with a pension or has significant assets. It is made shorter yet it he has some skill that he can fall back on in foreign ports, such as dentistry, medicine, marine electronics, diesel mechanics, etc.

It can be done. And in a whole lot less than a year. "John Peters" is starting out on his new life with a fully paid boat, debt-free, and with $20,000 in a money-fund account to draw from. Yet very few "vagabonds" have ever begun ocean voyages with anything approaching that—nor should you feel it necessary. If the men and women who have taken off for distant horizons aboard their own boats had waited until they had a bundle in the bank, few would have ever left port. The "Peters" example is only offered to show that the new way of life can be achieved in ways consistent with our ingrained concepts of responsibility and financial security—and in a remarkably short period of time.

It can be done. Easily.

7

How to Make a Living Afloat

Man's capacities have never been measured; nor are we judge of what he can do by any precedents, so little has been tried.

Whether you have followed the 1-Year Plan and are now cruising comfortably on a "stash" of fifty grand or so, or have sailed away with little more than beer money in the coffee can, there will eventually come a time when you either need money to continue cruising or simply want to beef up the kitty.

The cruising lifestyle can be a very economical one—or it can be extravagant. But even the low-budget voyages require a certain amount of money to maintain both the boat and its occupants. No matter how self-sufficient you are and how carefully planned the trip, the cruising sailor is going to run into busted engine parts, sudden medical emergencies, and corrupt port officials—to name but a few unpleasant surprises that become almost routine. In short, you need money to cruise, and for most of us, the day will come when the coin pile has shrunk to the point that a choice must be made: Earn some more money or head for home.

All too often, otherwise well-planned cruises end up on the rocks because of financial myopia. The cruiser-to-be has carefully planned out every detail of his new lifestyle but has neglected to prepare for the day when the money will run out. Money, after all, is an unpleasant subject to anyone fleeing the greenback-mad society we live in; somehow, it is felt, a living can be made through odd jobs here and there.

Let's get one thing very clear: You are very unlikely to finance continued cruising on "odd jobs." Quite simply, the market for labor is pretty cheap in most areas you will be cruising. In many countries, work permits are required for any meaningful employment, and these are almost impossible to obtain. Why give work to foreigners when your own country is suffering from unemployment? And where under-the-table jobs are available, the local natives are usually preferred anyway; they are more dependable, and they will work under conditions that no American or Canadian would accept. Even if you do land a one-shot job, it is going to pay peanuts because of the going market price on labor. This isn't the States: Your $10-an-hour job is going to pay thirty cents in New Caledonia. How many such jobs would it take to replace a $600 self-steering vane?

But there is a way. You *can* earn a living while cruising, thereby permitting you to extend your new lifestyle indefinitely. That way is to *prepare*. Just as you spent much of the 1-Year Plan preparing for the cruise by saving money, learning navigation, and gathering equipment, so you should spend it preparing yourself for earning an income while living aboard, no matter where you find yourself. In other words, learn a trade.

Now, this is not quite as difficult as it may sound at first. Keep in mind that there are usually no formal requirements as to education, licensing, or union affiliation when you are practicing marine electronics in the Marquesas. If you can fix the damn depthfinder, you will get paid twenty bucks! Nor is it necessary to become a recognized master of the craft you select. You need only make yourself better skilled and materially equipped than anyone else in the harbor—and that's not hard, in most places.

Of course, if you are one of the lucky ones, you already have a readily marketable skill. These include physicians', dentists', electronic technicians, electricians, carpenters, riggers, sailmakers, and mechanics, to name a few. In assessing your present skills, consider the needs of the native population. If you are cruising the rivers of Europe, there is little that you will be able to offer. Most cruising is done in the tropical areas, however, and, very conveniently, most countries in these areas have a continuing need—even on a short-term basis—for doctors, nurses, dentists, and, sometimes, teachers, engineers, and skilled farmers.

One well-known cruising sailor retired at an early age from his dental practice, and now sets up shop at every island he anchors at; for one or two days a week, he uses his case of dental tools on the local natives to pull out teeth, fill cavities, and treat gum problems—on a cash basis. Before you dismiss this because you are not a dentist, consider a crazy suggestion: Become one! First, try to rid yourself of the propaganda that has been instilled in your mind by such self-serving organizations as the American Dental Association. It does not require five or six years of college to polish enamel, fill a cavity, or pull out a tooth. Granted that an impacted wisdom tooth is another matter, there is nothing that says you cannot deal with the 90 percent of dental problems that do not require extensive surgery. Remember, dentistry used to be the job of barbers. Second, teach yourself the fundamentals of dentistry. This is not like "brain surgery self-taught"; it can be done—the same as plumbing can be self-taught. Except for the more complex problems—which you can learn to recognize—such as root canals and impacted teeth, you will find that dentistry is a fairly simple and easy trade. Despite the ADA, it *is* a trade, and a much simpler one to master than, say, marine electronics or carpentry. Third, get yourself a proper set of dental tools. These can be purchased used— often from a dental school or dental clinic. Include some pain killer, syringes, and antiseptic. Given a complete dental kit and a basic knowledge of dentistry, you will find yourself a very welcome individual in many remote areas of the world.

Any skill that deals with boat maintenance is a natural, and having that skill, you will be sought after almost anywhere cruising boats drop anchor. As we considered the needs of the indigenous populations you expect to meet, consider also the needs of the hundreds of fellow sailors you will encounter on your voyages. Most of them will have engines in their boats, sails on their masts, radio tranceivers in their cabins, and a whole lot more gear, most of which will eventually break down from the ravages of the ocean. In fact, the average yacht is a floating bucket of equipment needing repair—and, therefore, a source of income for anyone able to supply that need.

Consider taking up one of the skills so sought after among boat owners—electrician, electronic technician, carpenter, fiberglass repairman, rigger, sailmaker, diesel/gas mechanic, or refrigeration mechanic. Guaranteed: Master one of these crafts, and you will never again have to worry about how to muster up enough money to avoid heading back to the rat race.

Let's just take an example—an easy one. How long does it take to learn to repair sails? Granted that *making* sails is considerably more difficult (although certainly within the realm of your abilities), the repairing of sails takes little in the way of extensive knowledge or training. There are, of course, techniques to be learned and materials to become familiar with, but this can be done in your spare time within a matter of months. If you are fortunate enough to be near a professional sail loft, try to get a part-time job there so you can learn the skills first-hand; if they are not hiring, consider working for nothing as an investment in your future. In gaining the skills, you will acquire the sailmaker's tools and supplies; make sure you stock enough in the way of canvas, nylon, thread, needles, wax, etc., to last for years to come.

They may be impossible to find in some corners of the world. Most importantly, buy a good quality sailmaker's sewing machine—a special rig designed for stitching sails, which can be set up in a designated "shop" area of your boat. Now you are in business, and you will be surprised at how many boats anchored near you will have ripped sails that their owners have neither the equipment nor the ability to repair.

As with the sailmaker, so with the diesel mechanic, marine electrician, and so on: Your skills will be needed and will probably be at a premium. Any of these skills can be learned . . . to varying degrees of competence. But keep in mind that you are not trying to qualify for a license or pass any union requirements; you are just trying to learn how to become proficient enough at it to know what you are doing and to handle the majority of problems that will be presented to you. This can be accomplished in most cases by diligent application for a year or so, part-time. There will probably be trade schools near you, many of them offering evening extension classes; correspondence courses offer a less satisfactory but more convenient alternative. In some cases, the desired skills can be learned by taking only one or two very specialized classes, as, for example, with marine refrigeration or rigging.

With any skill, tools are critical. Whatever equipment you need to ply your trade should be bought at the quality level; it may well represent your economic lifeline, and it is going to have to survive the harsh conditions of salt water. Buy the best, even if used, and buy back-up equipment—there may be no replacements in the Galapagos Islands.

If you are just not inclined to make the effort of learning such a valuable sea-going skill, there may be the possibility of selling your services to neighboring vessels in other capacities. Cleaning hulls underwater, for example, can be accomplished with little more than a face mask, swim fins, and a stiff brush; of course, a scuba outfit helps. Teak decks, wood spars, and brass or bronze hardware all need care on any boat, particularly in the tropics. Keep in mind that your services will be more attractive if you supply the complete package to a potential customer—i.e., if you carry all the necessary teak oil and sealant, varnish, shellac, metal polish, etc. Keep in mind also that your services are considerably less valuable than those of a mechanic or electrician; the skipper is hiring you out of laziness, not need.

What about those less mechanically inclined? Fortunately, blue-water cruising offers some other possibilities for earning income. Let's look first at those that make use of the boat itself—chartering, interisland transportation and trade, fishing, and salvage.

Chartering is, of course, a possibility. But it is not the glowing answer to all financial needs that the neophyte sailor thinks it will be. If you are not averse to opening your home for strangers to live in, to being cooped up for days with people you may not like at all, to watching careless and thoughtless clients scuff up your topsides, spill coffee on the bunk cushions, and drop cigarettes on the teak, then you just might make it as a charter skipper. Maybe.

Remember some cardinal rules if you are going to try the chartering game. First, never, but *never*, offer your boat for bareboat charter; you, as skipper, go with the boat. This should be obvious, but many charterers are used to dealing with big companies in the relatively safe cruising areas of the Caribbean; these companies carry full insurance, do not have to live aboard their own boats, and are not dependent upon a boat for their existence. Second, have a clear understanding of the financial arrangements, preferably with payment in advance. It should also be understood in advance exactly what provisions are to be supplied by the skipper and what by the charterer; liquor, for example, may be expected by the client. Third, make the rules of conduct aboard your home very clear, including any feelings about intoxication, the use of soft-soled shoes, and handling of the boat.

Finding clients is usually a matter of using your imagination. Depending on your locale and cruising plans, you may be able to take out inexpensive advertisements in the local tourist-oriented publication. Placing notices on yacht club, marina, or harbor bulletin boards will often get results. If there are tourist resorts or hotels in the vicinity, a notice or two posted with permission may also prove successful.

If you plan on being in the area for six months or so, consider contacting the resort's management and proposing a deal: In return for their advertising and promoting your service to their guests, you fork over 25 percent of the fee. This is often an attractive offer to management, as the exclusive availability of a charter yacht adds prestige to the resort. They may, in fact, promote your charter operation quite extensively—*if* they are convinced you are capable and reliable.

Nevertheless, you should realize that chartering is no pot of gold at the end of the rainbow. The competition can be stiff; every other cruising sailor seems to be fattening the ship's kitty this way at some time or another. The income earned is often eaten up by advertising, fee sharing, provisioning, and increased maintenance. The local authorities may frown on your setting up business in their backyard; a license—with fees, insurance, and tons of paperwork—may be required, and possibly some under-the-table greasing of the wheels. The hassles with management, clients, and bureaucrats may be putting you right back into the rat race you supposedly escaped from. In short, chartering is not necessarily the easy answer-all that so many potential cruisers think it will be. But it can be done.

73

Transporting passengers and goods between islands is another possibility—at least, in those areas without adequate public ocean transportation. Of course, some of the same problems inherent in chartering apply with double force here. Passengers will trample over your boat with hard-soled shoes, cargo will be dropped, bureaucrats will offer never-ending roadblocks. But, again, it can be done, given the right kind of boat and the right kind of skipper.

You might want to look into becoming an "island trader." All romantic images aside, an astute businessman can do quite well by buying goods in one area where they are cheap and plentiful, and then reselling them on another island or in a whole different part of the world. If, for example, a cruising skipper were to stock up with a couple hundred pairs of assorted sizes of new or used Levi jeans at discount in Los Angeles, he could make quite a killing selling them in more remote corners of the globe. At this writing, used jeans can be bought at swap meets in the U.S. for a couple of bucks apiece; they sell for upwards of twenty dollars and more in some countries. Clothing, spare mechanical parts, and canned goods all represent items that can usually be purchased cheaply in one area for resale in another. The skipper does not have to put up with strangers aboard his vessel, although he may be faced with a nightmare of red tape when it comes to customs, import-export licenses, etc.—unless, of course, he wisely keeps a low profile.

Fishing is still another opportunity for the cruising sailor. Obviously, the boat must be suitable for this enterprise. Notably, it must have a hold for storing the fish and some method for keeping them cold—mechanical refrigeration, dry ice, or whatever. In the tropics, this can be a problem. Deep-sea fish are usually a desirable item anywhere, but you should always investigate your market before jumping in with both boots. Make sure there are buyers and that there is some way to reach them. Some communities have open-market places, where the fish can be sold directly; in others, contacting merchants or restaurants may prove rewarding. Again, keep in mind the ever-present possibility of bureaucratic interference.

For those not wishing or able to use their sailboats for commercial ventures, there are still ways to make a buck. One of the more pleasant of these is to give lectures or show motion pictures. In most of the places you will be visiting, the local people will be fascinated to learn of your travels and adventures. Whether you find yourself in New York or New Guinea, few of the natives will have ventured far beyond their own boundaries. Many of them would pay to be able to live vicariously some of your ocean-going experiences, particularly if your talk is accompanied by a slide show or even 8 or 16 mm. motion pictures. Not only can this be a source of income, but it is fun! And there is the added benefit of being able to meet a lot of the local people quickly— often resulting in invitations to dinners or parties. Obviously, a good still or movie camera would be helpful. Film, it should be noted, can be hard to find, expensive, and susceptible to damage by heat or humidity. Developing may also be a problem.

If you are not the public speaking type, consider becoming a traveling theatre magnate! In most of the more remote parts of the world, the showing of a Hollywood movie would be a big event—and worth, say, twenty-five cents admission. There are literally thousands of motion pictures available now for sale to the public at fairly low prices. Some classic hour-and-a-half movies can be bought for twenty dollars or so; cartoons, travelogues, and other "shorts" can be purchased for even less. Although many of them are still under copyright protection and sold for private viewing only, who is going to know in Rarotonga? A good used movie projector can be had for a hundred dollars, with an accompanying sound system for another hundred. A screen is not really necessary, and takes a lot of space; a white sheet can serve almost as well. A few extra light bulbs and spare parts should be brought along. Also, you'd better check about voltage and cycles available in your cruising areas. A transformer, run off a battery (DC) or generator (AC), may be needed. Again, protection of your now-valuable film from the elements must be kept in mind.

Finally, the individual planning to cruise indefinitely might consider writing for money—primarily magazine and newspaper articles but also books. What you are going to be doing is exactly what millions of other less imaginative people all around the world would like to be doing. Leading their dull lives of "quiet desperation," they devour articles about sailing and faraway romantic places. There is a market.

You should not think, however, that the market is an easy one. As with all areas of the publishing business, the magazines and newspapers have a whole lot more manuscripts submitted to them than they will ever put into print. Getting that first article accepted can be tough. It must be geared to the specific audience of the publication, be well-written, presented neatly, and probably accompanied by quality photographs. To put you a step or two ahead of others, then, a few simple rules to follow. First, understand what type of magazine or newspaper you are dealing with and the type of readership it has; a sailing article will not sell to *Powerboat* magazine. Second, write clearly and in plain English, avoiding the use of long words or a "flowery" or overly literate style. Third, type the article on plain white typing paper, double spaced, and leave margins on all four sides. The neatness and general professional appearance of your manuscript will immediately set it apart from over half of its competitors. Fourth, enclose a letter with the article briefly explaining what it is about and who you are. Fifth, try to photocopy the manuscript and submit the copies to a number of publishers at the same time; many of them profess to ignore "simultaneous submissions," but they do not, and your situation vis-à-vis the mail system requires it. Sixth, present a dozen good, clear photographs with captions, all protected by cardboard.

The going rate for articles varies, of course, with the length of the article, the reputation of the writer, and who the publisher is. Generally, a standard-sized article of, say, 2,500 words should pay anywhere from $200 to $800 or more. The rates are higher for the "biggies" such as National Geographic, but you should not waste postage on them. They are almost impossible to sell to, and most of their writing is done by staff. The following are good nationally published American markets for your articles:

75

Cruising World
Box 452
Newport, RI 02840
Attn: Executive Editor

Sailing
125 Main Street
Port Washington, WI 53074
Attn: Editor

Sail
38 Commercial Wharf
Boston, MA 02110
Attn: Editor

Sea and Pacific Skipper
CBS Publications
1499 Monrovia Ave.
Newport Beach, CA 92663

Yachting
1 Park Avenue
New York, NY 10016
Attn: Executive Editor

Yacht Racing/Cruising
North American Publishing Co.
Box 902
23 Leroy Ave.
Darien, CT 06820
Attn: Managing Editor

76

In additional to magazine articles, you might be interested in approaching a newspaper syndicate. These syndicates act as "word brokers," selling your writing to newspapers throughout the United States for a commission—usually 40 to 60 percent of the gross proceeds. Single articles may net anywhere from $50 to $500. If the syndicate likes your article and succeeds in selling it to various newspapers, they may be receptive to a continuing series of cruising articles—or possibly even to a regular column about your ongoing sailing adventures. If you land a column, of course, you have hooked the golden ring—a steady source of income no matter where your anchor lies. Some of the better syndicates you might want to contact with an article or two:

American Features Syndicate
964 3rd Avenue
New York, NY 10022
(Does not handle columns)

Community Features
Box 1062
Berkeley, CA 94703

Feature Associates
3334 Kerner Blvd.
San Rafael, CA 94901

King Features Syndicate
235 E. 45th St.
New York, NY 10017

Oceanic Press Service
Box 4158
North Hollywood, CA 91607

United Feature Syndicate
200 Park Avenue
New York, NY 10017

Universal Press Syndicate
4400 Johnson Drive
Fairway, KS 66205

Finally, the really energetic and ambitious may want to try his or her hand at writing a book. The same considerations as for articles hold true for book manuscripts: Know your market, write simply, and present your goods in a neat, professional form. Unlike magazine publishers, however, most book publishers prefer that you not submit a completed manuscript. Rather, in most cases you should forward an outline of the book, a sample chapter or two, and a covering letter explaining what the book is about and who you are (including, if possible, any published credits you may have). Again, do not feel reluctant to submit photocopies of the outline and sample chapter to a number of publishers at the same time.

The following book publishing companies are reputable firms and have reputations for publishing books dealing with cruising:

Cornell Maritime Press
Box 456
Centreville, MD 21617

Dodd, Mead, and Co.
79 Madison Ave.
New York, NY 10016

Doubleday and Co.
245 Park Avenue
New York, NY 10017

International Marine Publishing Co.
Camden, ME 04843

David McKay Co.
2 Park Avenue
New York, NY 10016

W. W. Norton and Co.
500 Fifth Avenue
New York, NY 10036

Sail
38 Commercial Wharf
Boston, MA 02110

As with any of the trades, writing will require tools. A good portable manual typewriter should be purchased. Sears makes a good model for around $150; good used typewriters can be picked up for $50 to $75. Plenty of typing paper, ribbons, envelopes, and cleaning and repair gear should be stocked, as these items are often hard to come by in remote areas.

So it can be done. You *can* make a living while cruising the oceans. But it usually means preparing yourself ahead of time. The best way is to learn a manual skill associated with boats, such as refrigeration mechanics or sailboat rigging. Whatever the proposed method for making a buck, you should realistically assess your chances of succeeding under the conditions and in the places you expect to be. Learn everything you can before you leave—you may not be able to after you leave— and then get the best quality tools of the trade you can afford. From there, it is usually just a question of imagination.

8

If You Can't Afford a Boat

Men will lie on their backs, talking about the fall of man, and never make an effort to get up.

It is difficult to imagine a situation where a man, a woman, or a family could not be able to buy a cruising sailboat with the exercise of diligence and discipline. If you have desire and imagination enough to want to change your present lifestyle so drastically, then you should be able to accomplish a matter as relatively simple as buying a boat. As has been seen in previous chapters, a simple application of the 1-Year Plan will result in a boat and a good-size cruising kitty to boot. Once you are on the way, numerous methods have been suggested for making a living while living aboard. And as the following chapters will indicate, there is a wide variety of good cruising boats available. You do not have to buy the biggest and most modern, an excellent used wooden sloop can bo obtained for under $10,000.

But perhaps you do not have the self-discipline to apply yourself economically for year or two. Perhaps you are simply anxious—in a hurry to get going *now*, unwilling to waste another year in the concrete-and-glass jungles. Or perhaps you just want to get out there and experience the cruising life for a year or two before dumping everything on an unknown proposition. Whatever the reason, the following are offered as alternatives to finding a better life afloat.

Basically, there are six recognized ways to long-term cruising without having your own boat:

1. *Chartering*
2. *Buying a boat in partnership with another individual or couple*
3. *Sharing running expenses with a boat owner*
4. *Paying your way as a passenger*
5. *Crewing*
6. *Getting a job yacht-sitting or delivering sailboats*

Let's take them one at a time.

Chartering has already been discussed in a previous chapter. It's a good way to find out if you like sailing and if you are compatible with the cruising life. The thousand dollars or so invested is a small amount compared to the time and money you will sink into the boat you buy—not to mention the ramifications of dumping your job, house, and lifestyle. On the other hand, chartering can quickly become prohibitively expensive if done on a long-term basis. At five hundred dollars a week, for example, the bill would quickly add up if you are talking about cruising for a year or more. Presumably, you are looking not for a vacation but for an entire new lifestyle; you intend to retire permanently to a life at sea. In such a case, chartering makes absolutely no sense at all.

If you want to try cruising for a year or two before committing yourself, then a private charter—i.e., an agreement with a private boat owner—might be feasible. A private owner who is not making use of his vessel may well release it for a year—fully insured, of course—for a whole lot less than a chartering company. That $500 per week boat would cost $26,000 a year (assuming no long-term discounts, of course); the private owner might "lease" the same type of vessel to you for $5,000 or so—particularly if he is not using it and it represents nothing but a continuing drain on his pocketbook. Of course, it is going to take some careful searching to find such a person. In all likelihood, he is not going to advertise—you will be suggesting the idea to him.

The second way to obtain a boat without putting out the full purchase price is simply to *buy it in partnership with another individual or couple*—or even with two or three other individuals or couples. Certainly, many such deals have been made, and there are right now dozens of sailboats cruising the world under this arrangement. And there are dozens of boats filled with people who have learned to hate one another.

That is the primary problem with joint ownership of a boat: Inevitably, it seems, the arguments begin. Not that there are not many

Sharing a boat with another couple is a good way to cut charter costs. (*The Moorings*)

vessels out there which are owned in partnerships and which have
been cruising happily for years. It happens. But it is probably the more
common experience to have the "partners" at each other's throats
within a matter of months. Why? Consider the physical circumstances
of living aboard a boat. The total living space is no larger than the
average kitchen. And this means that the "partners" will be forced to
live closely together—with no escape. Even when you are safely in
harbor, and flee to the mountains, you must eventually return to that
tiny little space with that person who has so got on your nerves. It gets

to the point where the way the other person combs his or her hair is enough to drive you up the wall!

Sound vaguely familiar to you married people? Well, multiply that by a hundred—by a thousand. You are living in a large apartment or house, with plenty of places to go and things to do. And you also have nature's own outlet for all that pent-up hostility—sex.

A partnership at sea incorporates all the bad points of marriage, with few of the benefits. But if you will not be talked out of it—if you are convinced that you and you buddy are terminally compatible—then go to it. If you do not yet have a partner, place ads in the yachting magazines or put up announcements at the marinas. Be forewarned, however, that this random way of selecting a close living partner is a pretty poor way of guaranteeing compatibility no matter how carefully you screen those answering.

The third way of cruising without investing a pile in a boat is to *share the operating expenses with a boat owner*. In other words, you agree to become crew in exchange for putting up money to offset the daily costs of food, diesel, slip fees, maintenance, and so on. The exact arrangements differ, of course, from situation to situation. In some cases, the sharing expenses can amount to a skippered charter, with the "crew" paying a large fixed weekly or monthly sum. In more satisfactory deals, the crew is putting up money only as it is shown to be needed; this will sometimes amount to as little as a hundred bucks a month.

The same problems pertain here as with partnerships, of course: the skipper and crew can get on each other's nerves very quickly, particularly if you have hooked up with a Captain Bligh-type. But at least you are free to leave the arrangement with no economic loss—unlike the partner who has ten or twenty grand tied up in the boat.

Again, such deals as can be found can be found by advertising. The other side advertises too. Skippers looking for a crew to share running expenses are not too uncommon, and they will place notices on bulletin boards or ads in newspapers or magazines. The following, taken from the current issue of one national yachting magazine, represent the type:

CREW WANTED. Island-hopping cruise in Bahamas. 41' ketch. Diving, exploring, etc. Share expenses. 2 weeks minimum. May-June-July. (Phone number).

One year Boston/Caribbean trip being planned. Interested? Write: (address).

PRIVATE SAILING YACHT cruising Caribbean en route South Pacific. M/F berths available. Share expenses. (address).

Some of these can be pretty good deals, offering short-term cruising exposure at bargain prices; many develop into longer term arrangements. However, it should be mentioned that some of these advertisements are worthless come-ons, designed either to attract charter customers to unlicensed skippers or to obtain slave labor who will pay charter rates. In dealing with any skipper who advertises for crew like this, you should ask yourself why he had to advertise, i.e., why were there not dozens of individuals obtainable through word-of-mouth who would have jumped at the chance?

Four: *Paying your way as a passenger*. Basically, this differs very little from sharing expenses as crew. If there is a difference, it will be that less is expected in the way of work and the money will be a fixed sum rather than a percentage of expenses as they occur. But these arrangements differ, and the lines between informal private chartering, expense-share crewing, and paying as a passenger are fluid.

The fifth course is to *sign on as crew*. This is considerably different from sharing expenses as crew. Here we are talking about landing a *job*, a full-time position as, presumably, a general deckhand aboard a large yacht. In no way will you be considered a quasi passenger or partner, as with someone informally sharing expenses. You will be expected to put in a full day and may end up working twice as hard as you ever did on shore—sanding, varnishing, cooking, polishing, painting, etc. The pay is usually low—often no more than fifty or a hundred dollars a week—because there are so many applicants who want to live and work aboard a yacht. The vessel's destination, if any, will be completely up to the owner, and your involvement in the daily life at sea will be menial. With rare exceptions, such situations are no fun at all and are difficult to find, but they do offer the chance to experience life at sea, with no financial investment.

If you are a couple considering such an alternative, do not be discouraged by the fact that there are two of you. Husband-and-wife teams are relatively common as hired hands, the wife traditionally serving as cook while the husband does deckhand chores. In fact, husband-and-wife teams are often preferred and actively sought by yacht owners. The theory is that such people tend to be safer and more stable than solo hands—that is, they are less likely to jump ship at the first port, or hijack the boat in the middle of the night.

Sixth and last: *yacht-sitting or yacht delivery*. Altogether, not bad ways to live aboard with little or no overhead. Yacht-sitting is simply that—living on board a boat while the owner is away. This is done by the owner for two very good reasons. First, it helps ensure security (the presence of an individual or couple living aboard will reduce the chances of theft, vandalism, or damage from natural causes). Second, the condition of the boat is maintained. One of the agreements of the arrangement will probably be that the liveaboard perform routine maintenance on the boat—scrub the decks, bleach and oil the teak, polish the brightwork, and so on.

Of course, this does not usually get you onto the open seas; it means simply that you sit on a boat at anchor or in a slip. But some arrangements include the opportunity to go out with the owner when he does decide to sail the boat. If nothing else, however, it will give you a bit of a feel for living aboard a sailboat. And you may make valuable contacts at your anchorage or marina—people who are planning a long cruise and who are looking for compatible crew. Also, if the boat you are sitting is anchored in Tahiti or Martinique, there are worse ways to spend your time.

Yacht delivery is a different matter. Many skippers, boat manufacturers, or marine brokers want to get a boat from, say, Annapolis to San Diego. Rather than paying the exorbitant costs of shipping a 40-foot yacht by truck or rail, they will simply hire an experienced skipper to sail it there for a whole lot less. The shipper usually pays a flat rate to the delivery skipper; in some cases, separate compensation for food and gear will be made.

Fair warning: Most of these deliveries are made by licensed, professional skippers or agencies. Their advertisements can be seen in most national yachting magazines. The reasons for this are clear: The owner/manufacturer/broker wants to ensure that the individual is trustworthy and experienced. And the insurance policy on the vessel is probably invalid without a licensed professional supervising the delivery; most delivery agencies are bonded or carry their own policies.

Yet there are opportunities here. Your chances are poor with a broker or manufacturer, but there are owners out there who will entrust their boat to the right person for delivery. These situations will not be discovered in advertisements; they are found, usually, through word-of-mouth. The best bet, then, is to ask around the marinas, anchorages, and yacht clubs and to keep your eyes and ears open. When you do find an owner who wants his boat delivered, he is not going to turn it over to you without being confident of your experience and abilities. Assuming you are fairly new at cruising, the more realistic approach is to solicit a position as crew to the delivery skipper. Usually, the owner and delivery skipper will both be happy to have more crew aboard to help—provided that the applicant seems a decent sort. Be prepared to offer references; the yachting world has seen a veritable epidemic of hijackings in recent years—skippers murdered at sea by their crews and the vessel commandeered for the drug-smuggling trade.

Perhaps one of the best ways to land a spot on a delivery job is to look for long-distance yacht races. The Transpac from California to Hawaii is a good example; the California-Tahiti race is another. These races are one-way: They are designed to take advantage of the prevailing winds and currents. Once at the final destination, the skipper is faced with returning his sleek ocean greyhound to its home port—against the wind and waves. Some skippers are short on time, others tired, still others simply unwilling to fight back to home. The same goes with many of their crew. If you make yourself known and available at docks at the end of the race, and if possible, at the inevitable postrace parties, you are likely to land a position crewing one of the racing machines back to its home.

85

Another possibility is to contact one of the professional delivery agencies, offering to serve as crew for no pay on one of their jobs. It is unlikely, but you never can tell. Their advertisements, as mentioned before, can be found in any national yachting magazine. Marine brokers and manufacturers can also be contacted for the names and locations of reputable delivery skippers.

You *can* cruise, whether you own a boat or not. Like everything else, it only requires a little imagination and a little more perseverance.

Part 3
Buying the Boat

9

Which Boat for You?

Heaven is under our feet as well as over our heads.

(Author's note: The following is, of necessity, a very brief discussion of the various design considerations in the selection of a cruising boat. The reader should certainly read more comprehensive works on the subject—listed in the Bibliography herein—and consult with experts before determining what basic design he desires.)

The decision has been made: You and your family have decided to take the big step, chucking the dreary miseries of life ashore for the freedom and adventure of a new and better life cruising the oceans of the world. Your house is up for sale, the 1-Year Plan is in operation, and everyone in the family is enthusiastically preparing for the great adventure. And you are about to enter a new and exciting stage in getting ready for this new life—finding your boat.

The selection of a boat that is right for you and your family is a critical process: It will be your home for the next few years—possibly for the rest of your life. The wisdom of that selection—the suitability of the boat for your unique needs and abilities—will have a considerable impact on the eventual success of your plans; the wrong boat can mean continuous troubles and frustrations, while the right one will be a source of unending pleasure. As the future skipper, it is your duty to find a boat that will accommodate your family comfortably, perform well in the conditions you expect to meet, and provide an acceptable degree of safety in almost any weather the seas can throw at you.

In some ways, you will find shopping for your boat much like it was shopping for your first house. Is the new home large enough for the family? Are there any structural problems, such as dry rot? In what condition is the plumbing and electrical wiring? Is the insulation sufficient for expected extremes in temperature? Has the home been built strongly enough to withstand the most severe of local weather conditions? These and other questions will apply in their own way to the selection of the proper boat.

Yet the similarities between house- and boat-shopping are limited. The house is on solid land. Any necessary repairs can be done by local experts, and the structure can be evacuated at any time. Put quite simply, the house will not sink in the middle of the ocean with all hands aboard; rarely will the nature or quality of the house's design and construction be critical to the safety of its occupants. The opposite is true for the cruising boat owner: Both the design and the quality of construction can literally be a matter of life or death. The safety and comfort of your family is directly tied to the integrity of the boat you've chosen, and facing a 60-knot gale in the North Atlantic is no time to be having second thoughts about whether the rigging will hold up. In such a situation, you and your loved ones are stuck on board, unable to leave for a safer location, unable to call in experts to repair structural flaws. The die will be cast: Either the boat will prove sturdy and reliable, or it will not.

Fine. So how do you go about locating the boat that is a comfortable home for you and your family, a safe, seaworthy vessel able to bring you safely through whatever the seas will offer?

Narrowing the Field: Basic Design

Perhaps you've already gone browsing through the local yacht anchorages, looking for the perfect boat. Or maybe you've been poring over the thousands of advertisements in yachting magazines. If so, then you've been confronted by a staggering variety of vessels from which to choose. In selecting a house, the choice of design may be between colonial or ranch, three bedrooms or four, one story or two. But the range of boat designs is vastly greater: Is it to be a power boat or sail? diesel powered or outboard gas engine? a two-masted ketch or a singlemasted sloop? full or fin keel? aft cabin or twin? a catamaran or a monohull? fiberglass or wood? . . . and the decisions go on seemingly without end—decisions that will have a direct effect on the success of your new adventure.

You must first decide what basic design is best suited for you. After considering the merits and drawbacks of the competing designs, you will begin to narrow the field down to a particular type of boat that will best fulfill your needs and expectations.

Sail versus Power

The first decision to be made is whether your new home will be a motorboat or a sailboat. Obviously, the author is strongly biased toward the sailboat as the ideal vessel for ocean cruising, and there are a number of very good reasons for this.

To begin with, the wind doesn't cost you a nickel; it's there for the taking. The price of gasoline or diesel, on the other hand, continues to skyrocket into the atmosphere. It doesn't take much mental arithmetic to figure that the expenses of motoring from, say, San Diego to the Galapagos Islands at a consumption rate of two gallons of fuel per hour would quickly put a big dent in anyone's pocketbook.

And once safely moored in the Galapagos, is there any guarantee of finding another fuel fix? With the present vagaries of man's increasing energy shortages, no skipper can safely predict that gas or diesel will be readily available—particularly not in such remote locations as the Galapagos Islands. Sure, the wind dies down sometimes for days at a stretch. But it will always return, eventually. Gas or diesel, however, may not be obtainable for months—and in some remote anchorages, never.

And where does all this fuel go? It's stored in the boat, of course— large volumes of heavy cargo taking away from the already limited space available for storage of needed equipment and supplies. And all those gallons of fuel are right under your bunk. How do you like the idea of your family floating across the Pacific on a tank of highly explosive gasoline?

For some, the simple aesthetics of sailing versus motoring is determinative. The indescribable feeling of the wind whistling through the rigging, the blue-green waves lapping rhythmically at the hull as the bow knifes silently through the water—this is what it's all about for many sailors. Compare that to the stinking smell of gasoline permeating everything about you and the maddeningly steady thud-thud of the engine turning over, drowning out all harmony with the peaceful environment of the seas.

But all such considerations aside, the sailboat is preferable to the motorboat for one very simple reason: It is infinitely more seaworthy. Ocean voyages have, of course, been safely made by small powerboats, and they will continue to be made. But the fact remains that the vast majority of ocean voyaging has been accomplished by sailboats. And this is because of the inherent seaworthiness of the sailboat design.

By "seaworthiness" I mean the ability of a boat to perform on the oceans and to withstand the various forces of nature acting upon it. Almost any boat—power or sail— can cruise across the Chesapeake Bay on a calm day in reasonable safety. But what if you are in the mid-Pacific when a gale arrives in full force? Then a given vessel's inherent seaworthiness depends essentially upon three factors: control, stability, and structural strength.

The sailboat is designed to harness the forces of nature in such a way as to keep her in balance. The lead ballast in her keel, for example, acts as a countering force to the increased angle of the boat as her sails fill with stronger winds; as the boat heels over in a storm, the effective weight of the keel—together with increased "spilling" of wind from the sails as they dip further from the vertical—increases to the point where the boat physically will lean over no further. In any given weather situation, the laws of nature will operate to find a correct angle of heel for a given sailboat. And, unless there is a temporary "knock-down" from some rogue wave (in which case she will automatically right herself) the sailboat is almost impossible to flip over.

You've found an angle of heel determined by a combination of wind and boat design. Note that that angle will tend to remain fairly steady. That means that while there will be some pitching as with any boat—a fore-and-aft hobby-horse motion—there will be relatively little rolling from side to side. Result: increased stability, better control, and less strain on the boat—and its occupants.

Because of the sailboat's keel design, she will tend to *track*. This means that she will have a strong tendency to move forward in a straight line, as the combined forces of wind against sail and water against keel will force her into a track. Again, increasing stability and control. In fact, most sailboats can be rigged to steer themselves because of this tracking quality. Many sailboats, additionally, have what is termed a *weather helm*; that is, if left unattended, they will slowly pull up bow into the wind and come to a stop, with sails flapping emptily; this predictable characteristic can be very helpful in emergency situations.

As a result of the sailboat's design adapting to the forces of nature, rather than fighting them, the skipper has a safer, stronger, more easily controlled vessel in his hands. By contrast, the motorboat is poorly suited to blue-water cruising because of its failure to adapt. Quite simply, the forces of wind and water are working against the boat rather than with it. There is nothing in the powerboat's design to maintain stability and control other than such man-made, and very fallible, objects as engine and rudder; should the engine fail (a not uncommon occurrence in storms), the boat is completely helpless. There is nothing in nature to keep the powerboat going in a straight line, nothing to keep it from rolling uncontrollably, nothing to prevent it from flipping over, and, once over, nothing to bring it back to an upright position. In short, the forces of nature are operating to make the boat unstable, difficult to control, and subject to increased structural strain.

Get a sailboat.

The Multihulls v. the Monohulls

The next question is: What about those fast, sexy catamarans? And this brings up one of many areas of violent disagreement between members of the nautical fraternity: Which is better suited for blue-water cruising, the monohull or the multihull?

Let's first define the breed. The monohull is, of course, the traditional form of sailboat, the classic single hull. The multihulls, however, consist of two or three hulls joined together by a cabin and deck; in the case of a catamaran, two equal hulls, and in the case of a trimaran, a large central hull flanked on each side by smaller hulls. Although these multihulls have found favor in cruising circles relatively recently, they are based upon design concepts as old as the ancient Polynesian mariners. That they could have carried men from the South Pacific over thousands of miles of open ocean to Hawaii hundreds of years ago says something of their merit. Yet the question remains: Is the design as good as, or better than, the western monohull?

Consider the strengths of the multihull. First, they are fast—often, very fast. In most racing conditions, a good catamaran will clean the monohull skipper's clock. A second benefit is that the multihull will sail better in lighter wind conditions than will the deeper-hulled traditional sailboat.

Another consideration is greater initial stability. Because of the lateral positioning of the twin or triple hulls, the multihull will sail under normal conditions without heeling over in a breeze. This can increase speed because less wind will spill from the sails, and at the same time it offers a more level, and thus comfortable, boat to live aboard at sea.

Finally, the multihull generally offers more living space than a monohull of equal length. This is due to the greater beam—lateral

93

space—and to the fact that each of the hulls can be used for living area and storage.

So why isn't everyone cruising on cats or trimarans? Because there are drawbacks to the multihull designs, although rabid cat skippers will vehemently deny it. To begin with, the multihulls can be difficult to tack (change course) under certain conditions. Tacking must be done quickly and decisively, or there is a risk of coming to a dead stop as the bow swings into the wind. This can be embarrassing, if not downright dangerous under certain circumstances.

94

Secondly, while the multihulls have high *initial* stability, their ultimate stability is very poor. In other words, it is very difficult to tip a cat or trimaran beyond a relatively level angle of sail, but once that angle is passed, the boat will quickly flip over. And here is the third catch to the multihull: Once over on her back, she will not right herself. The worst of conditions in a raging sea will knock any sailboat over. The monohull, being self-righting by design, will quickly pop back up; the multihull will lie on her back like a turtle, mast pointed to the ocean's floor.

Finally—and this is a point strenuously denied by many cat men— the design of the multihull increases structural stress. With the traditional sailboat, the hull is a single unit immersed in water; the primary stress operating on the hull comes directly from the sea, and this will be minimized by good hydrodynamic design. But the multihull has two or three units in the water, connected by cross-members; any stress from the sea against one hull will be transmitted to the other through the structural connections. As a result, the hulls of the cat or trimaran are working against each other, flexing and twisting from the stresses of the sea—and translating this external stress into internal stress as well. Eventually, heavy stress from pounding seas on the multihull's structure can result in the boat breaking apart. And that can be an unpleasant experience.

Cat men will point out that more lives have been lost at sea aboard monohulls than aboard multihulls. But this eludes a simple fact: Monohulls vastly outnumber multihulls. A higher *percentage* of multihulls have disappeared at sea.

The multihull has its strengths as it does its weaknesses, and there is no shortage of religious adherents to both sides of the argument. If you are seriously interested in a cruising cat or trimaran, there are many excellent reference books extolling their virtues; some are listed in the bibliography.

For now, we will assume you're taking the safe and proven course: the traditional monohull.

How Many Poles?

And now we come to one of the favorite subjects for argument among seagoing men: What is the best rigging for a sailing boat? Is it the ketch? The sloop? Or maybe the schooner? And should it be Marconi—or gaff-rigged?

For our purposes, we will dismiss such esoteric designs as square-riggers and Chinese junks—though they are proven blue-water sailers—and concentrate on the more practical and far more common styles of rigging. As with almost anything in the nautical world, there is violent disagreement as to the relative merits of each design. The racing skipper will extol the virtues of the high-masted Marconi sloop, while the old-timer will spit on anything but a gaff-rigged ketch or schooner. Yet there is enough agreement to make certain generalizations as to the strengths and weaknesses of each. And based on these, you will be able to find the rigging design best suited to your needs.

First, a brief word about the Marconi versus the gaff rig. The Marconi is the conventional triangular sail, aligned fore-and-aft; it is often referred to as the Bermudan rig. It is by far the most common sailing rig, found on perhaps 90 percent of all modern western sailboats. Its simplicity of design and proven efficiency are good reason for its present popularity. The gaff rig, on the other hand, is the traditional sail arrangement, common in years past but now seen primarily on "character" boats, usually of schooner or ketch design. Rather than a triangular sail, it is four-sided, with the upper side supported by a boom, smaller than the lower boom, called a *gaff*. When the sail is lowered, the gaff is brought down and rested on the lower boom. The primary benefit of the gaff rig is that a larger amount of upper sail is presented to the wind; this can be helpful when the boat is in deep troughs between waves. However, the overall efficiency is questionable as against the Marconi rig, particularly when sailing close into the wind, and the added weight and gear are decided disadvantages.

For most purposes, you will be better off with the Marconi rig.

Now to consider the mast arrangement. The simplest and by far most common of the conventional sailboat designs is the *sloop*, with Marconi sails. The sloop is a sailing vessel with a single mast. Its primary benefits are simplicity and a closer possible angle of sailing to windward. Having a single mast, the sloop will have only two sails to contend with—the main and the jib. This reduces the number of sails that must be carried aboard as well as the amount of lines, winches, and tackle that can be potential sources of failure. Also, with only two sails to work, the crew will expend less labor in changing and trimming them.

A McGinnis-designed, Japanese built 35-foot wooden sloop that is being cruised around the world by an elderly couple.

A Cape Dory 28—a solid, full-keeled Alberg-designed cruiser.

The primary strength of the sloop, however, is its ability to *point* high to the wind. This simply means that it can sail at a closer angle to the direction from which the wind is coming. No boat can sail directly into the wind, but the sloop can come closer to it than any other design. This may not seem like a very important advantage, but rest assured that it is. Trying to make a port against the wind may take twice as long aboard a ketch because of the wider tacks necessary. And when you are fighting a storm that is trying to blow you onto a reef, the difference in tacking angle can prove critical.

The second most common basic sailboat design is the *ketch*. This is a two-masted vessel, with the main mast somewhat forward of mid-ships, and the mizzen mast to the rear of it but just forward of the tiller or wheel. The ketch has found particular favor among world cruisers, as its strengths lend it to a wide variety of conditions, including rough water. Because of the two masts and three sails, there is a wider variety of possible balanced sail combinations: dropping the main and sailing under jib and mizzen, for example, or dropping the mizzen and sailing her like a sloop. Another obvious advantage to the ketch is that since there are two masts, a single dismasting in a storm need not be disastrous—the boat can still make way on the remaining mast, much as with a twin-engined airplane with one engine gone. Finally, the sails aboard a ketch will each be proportionately smaller than those on a sloop—although the *total* sail area may be greater—and, thus, more easily handled. While you may not think this to be a major benefit right now, you will when you try to drop or *reef* your first mainsail in a raging storm.

Above: The Pearson 365, a fine, lighter-displacement cruising ketch. Right: A wooden Tahiti ketch, precursor of the currently popular double-ended cruising boats.

As with any design, the ketch also has its disadvantages. As mentioned earlier, the ketch will not sail as close-hauled to the wind as a sloop. There is considerable disagreement, however, as to which is the faster on other points of sail. Very generally speaking, the sloop will do well in lighter airs, while the ketch will outperform her rival in rough seas—partly because of being able to safely keep up more sail area. There is, of course, more gear and sails to handle and, therefore, to go wrong; simplicity is always a prime consideration in ocean cruising. Finally, the ketch may experience problems when "running"—that is, sailing with the wind coming from the stern. This is because of the possibility of the blanketing effect: The mizzen sail will block much of the wind from reaching the more powerful main and jib, thus reducing speed. With the wind at your back, you may have to drop the mizzen, reducing the total sail area to less than the sloop's.

The *cutter* is a third type of sailboat design—and one which has found increasing favor in recent years. Basically, the cutter is identical to a sloop, except that it has *two* sails foreward of the mast; while the sloop has only a jib, the cutter has a jib and a second sail alongside of it, called a "staysail". The cutter seems to combine some of the benefits of the ketch and sloop: It has increased speed and adaptability from having more sails, yet it is capable of pointing close to windward.

Yet another design is the *yawl*. This is a sailboat with the main mast located slightly forward of midships, as with the ketch, but with its mizzen to the *rear* of the tiller or wheel—usually, at the aft edge of the cockpit, with the boom extending out beyond the stern. Generally, the yawl's mizzen will be smaller than a ketch's, although its mainsail may be larger. Although notable world cruises have been made aboard yawls—John Guzzwell's tiny *Trekka* is a fine example—the design has generally not found widespread favor, and you will find relatively few such boats sailing the oceans today. Many experts doubt whether the small size of the mizzen sail is worth the expense and complications of having the second mast, particularly when it acts to blanket a following wind from the main and jib. And because the mizzen boom extends aft of the stern, installation and operation of a self-steering wind vane—almost mandatory equipment for world cruising—becomes very difficult.

Finally, there is the old classic design that warms the heart of every traditionalist—the *schooner*. This design uses two masts, but with the main mast aft (in front of the steering mechanism) and the shorter mast forward. This gives the boat a rakish effect, particularly when accompanied, as old schooners often are, with gaff rigging. Unfortunately, the schooner design has little to recommend it for

98

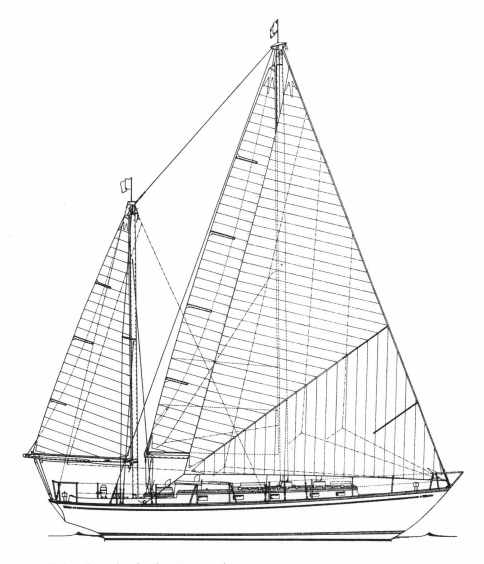

The sail plan of a modern ketch. (*Mason Yachts*)

anyone other than the diehard romantic. It has the drawbacks of the ketch, with few of the benefits. It is more difficult to balance, has the poorest angle of sail to windward of any design, and has all the problems inherent in increased complexity of design.

As in other areas of yacht design, sailboat masts and rigging continue to have radical new concepts and materials applied—often successfully. One of the most interesting recent developments is the

100

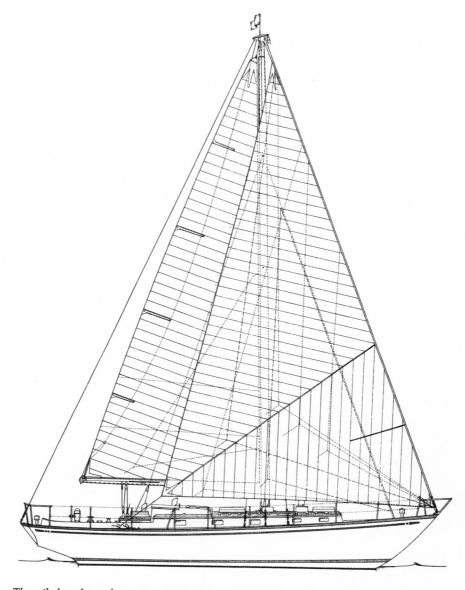

The sail plan of a modern cutter rig. Note the overlapping forward sails. (*Mason Yachts*)

unstayed mast. Developed by Pioneer Yachts, the masts are constructed of graphite—an extremely light yet strong material—and require neither stays nor shrouds. They are completely unsupported above the deck. Obviously, the simplicity of such a design offers tremendous benefits; a jungle of wires is gone and with it the source of constant equipment failure.

So the field is narrowing. Do you want the simplicity and windward abilities of the sloop? Are you going to choose the adaptability of the ketch? Or will you opt for the combined benefits of the cutter?

It's your decision.

Hull Design

All right, let's say you've decided that a ketch is the right boat for your needs. That's fine for the rigging. But what about the most important part of the boat, the part that keeps you and your family from the deep blue? What kind of a *hull* do you want?

This can be broken down into three basic considerations: materials, shape, and keel-rudder configuration. Each of these three decisions will have long-lasting effects. For, without a doubt, the quality of your hull's design and construction will have a greater bearing on the type of sailing and the degree of safety that you will experience on your cruise than any other single factor.

Hull Materials

There are four commonly used materials that can be employed in constructing the all-important hull: wood, steel, ferrocement, and fiberglass. As with almost everything else in yacht design, each has its unique strong points and each has its weaknesses.

Wood is the age-old method of building sailing vessels, although its use today is relatively rare. Nevertheless, there are professional builders still putting out beautiful yachts built of teak, oak, iroko, or other suitable wood—either of the classic plank construction or of the newer steam-bent or laminated methods. Certainly, the wooden sailboat has its advantages. If properly built, wood is strong while at the same time having a beneficial degree of flexibility. In the warmer climates it will "breathe," preventing excessive condensation inside the boat. It is a relatively inexpensive method of construction, unless exotic woods are used; an older wooden boat can be bought for half the price of its used fiberglass counterpart. And, very importantly, repairs can more easily be made under a wider variety of circumstances. If you run your new home up on a reef in the Marquesas, you may find that wood is the only material available to patch up that gaping hole in the hull; and when was the last time you worked with ferrocement or a welding rod?

On the debit side, however, wood hulls have a number of irritating qualities. They will get dry rot—a festering disease that will

destroy a boat from the inside out. They will get teredo worms—
particularly in the tropics, where the slimy devils can sink a small
sailboat within a matter of weeks. They can split and crack and begin
disintegrating under the attack of sun and salt water, if they are not
constantly repainted. And changes in climate can cause wood planks to
shrink, forming gaping holes for sea water to pour through. A lot of
trouble, wood.

Steel has the great benefit of strength. It's going to take one heck
of a blow to cause any serious damage to a well-built steel hull. For
some sailors, with visions of coral reefs or playful whales dancing in
their minds, this is enough. But the drawbacks to steel construction
will probably outweigh the benefits in the final analysis. As already
mentioned, working on steel repairs can be difficult or impossible. A
second problem is that a steel hull can prove uncomfortable in the
tropical climates so popular to sailing men, acting almost like a Dutch
oven. But the main weakness of steel is its chemical reaction with the
salt water environment. No matter how often you paint the inside and
outside of the hull, rust is going to appear; left unattended, the rust
will eventually render the boat structurally unsafe. On top of that,
there is a continuous galvanic and electrochemical reaction going on
underwater, which can result in a disintegrating propeller, weakened
hull, and other nightmares. Still interested in steel?

As to ferrocement, the main advantages are two: It's cheap and
it's easy. It is also fairly strong and impervious to organic or
electrolytic degeneration. Ferrocement is a relatively new boat-building
material, having caught on mainly among the backyard do-it-
yourselfers because it doesn't cost much and it requires little in the way
of special skills or equipment. As a result, many, if not most, of the
ferrocement boats in the water today are home-built. Obviously, this
means that if you are shopping for a used boat, be particularly wary of
those with ferrocement hulls; it's a good, tough material, and many
backyard projects turn out to be beautiful, seaworthy vessels, but at
least as many are disasters. Advice: Stay away from ferrocement hulls,
despite their strong points.

Okay, so that leaves fiberglass. While not the favorite of the
purists, this petrochemical derivative is easily the most prevalent
material used in building sailboats today. The vast majority of yachts
coming from commercial yards are made of glass. It is expensive and
difficult to work with should you require extensive repairs. But
consider the advantages of this modern material: It doesn't leak,
doesn't rust, experiences no galvanic or electrochemical action, is
impervious to worms, can't rot, and will apparently last indefinitely.
Properly constructed, fiberglass is plenty strong, and a new

construction process using sandwiched layers of foam makes it even stronger. Kits for minor repair work are small and lightweight, and maintenance of a glass hull is the next thing to nonexistent.

If you can afford it, get a boat with a fiberglass hull. If you can't, there are a lot of good, solid wood boats to be found—and for a whole lot less money.

Hull Shape

There are almost as many different hull configurations as there are sailboat designs, and not a month passes without some naval architect coming up with what he feels to be an improved hull shape. And make no mistake: The shape of the hull will have more to do with "seakindliness" of your boat than any other single factor.

Let's consider the effect of hull configuration on performance. In any sailboat, we want speed, comfort, bouyancy, stiffness, and ease of handling. Speed is largely determined by the boat's length at the waterline and the amount of sail presented to the wind. But it is also determined by the shape of the hull—a shape that will offer the least resistance to the flow of water along its sides. Naval architects spend a good hunk of their lives testing various hull shapes in water tanks, and there is no agreement yet on the ideal form. However, the cruising sailor must temper the search for speed with other requirements as well.

The needs of comfort—and there is a direct correlation at sea between comfort and safety—dictate that the boat have sufficient beam and draft to her for living space and stability, while streamlined enough to cut through the seas rather than wallowing, pounding, rolling, or pitching unduly. A seasick or exhausted crew is working at a dangerously low level of efficiency, and that is when accidents happen. A properly designed hull will provide sufficient living area and will maximize the stability of the vessel under the prevailing weather and wind conditions.

Bouyancy is an obvious requirement, but the bouyancy provided by the hull must be more than just sufficient to keep the boat afloat. It must permit the vessel to ride over the seas rather than plowing through them. Even when the boat is heavily loaded with equipment and supplies, she should lift above the waves so that no large amounts of water are taken aboard. Such bouyancy is obtained through a combination of lightweight structural materials, sufficiently high freeboard (the distance from the waterline to the top of the hull), properly designed sheer (the outward-flowing contour of the hull), and sufficient overhang at the bow and stern.

There has been considerable disagreement over the best configuration for a boat's stern. The *transom* advocates claim that a transom— a gracefully squared-off stern, often in the shape of a wine glass—is more attractive and will lift the stern up and over waves as they approach from the rear, thus preventing the vessel from being *pooped*, or buried under a following sea. The *double-enders*, on the other hand, insist that the canoe-like stern will separate the following seas, rather than offering a squared-off target. Neither side has succeeded in disproving the arguments of the other; transoms are much the more common type of stern, but double-enders are rapidly gaining in popularity among world cruisers. Take your pick.

Stiffness of the hull is another desirable trait. A "stiff" vessel will be one that will hold fairly steady in a blow, rather than be knocked about laterally by waves and wind. This is accomplished by a combination of wide beam, deep draft, heavy keel, and solid structural sections.

Finally, ease of handling is primarily determined by the balance of the hull and the boat's stiffness. The forward section of the hull should be perfectly matched to the after section, so that whether the boat is upright or heeled over she will steer easily and responsively and tend to track or come to weather without anyone at the helm.

The ideal hull is one that has a low wetted surface with a fairly light displacement (weight of water displaced when the boat is afloat). The bilges (sides) should be beamy and hard (flat) enough to attain initial stability and sufficient speed, yet slack (rounded) enough to permit an easy motion at sea, without pounding.

The ability to discern the proper hull configuration for your purposes is a matter probably best left to experts. It's difficult for even the knowledgeable sailor to be able to predict a sailboat's qualities from simply looking at the hull; however, the better-known designs of boats will have acquired reputations for their performance—or lack of it. At the very least, one basic approach seems usually to hold true: If a hull's lines appear graceful and pleasing to the eye, there is a good chance she's quick enough and seaworthy.

Keel and Rudder Configurations

You are going to find three basic types of keels from which to choose—the fin keel, the hollow keel with internal ballast, and the hollow keel with bolted-on external ballast. Again, each design has its own peculiar strengths and weaknesses.

The fin keel is usually made of metal and is bolted on to the bottom of the boat's hull. It is comparatively thin and small and, consequently, causes less drag through the water. Result: The boat will

Top: The Cal 27, a compact version of the popular Cal 29 light-displacement cruising sailboat, which has a transom stern. Above: An example of the modern heavy-displacement double-ender—the Tayana 37.

be faster and more maneuverable. Almost all racing sailboats have fin keels, but there are a few cruisers also opting for their speed and quick handling. Yet the drawbacks are enough to keep them in the minority among blue-water sailors. Fins have no internal space for a bilge sump or fuel/water tanks, they require heavy reinforcement where they join the hull—and even then may be structurally weak—and they are less stable than the deep-keel designs.

The hollow keel can be of any number of designs, from a short and shallow keel that is no larger than a fin to a deep and broad extension of the hull that runs from the bow all the way back to the stern. Very generally speaking, the deeper and longer the keel is, the more stable the vessel will be, but, as usual, at a cost—the boat will also be less responsive at the helm, tending to plow sluggishly straight ahead. This is a wonderful asset in the middle of a gale but can be tricky when you are trying to maneuver through a crowded harbor.

The hollow keel has the added advantage of providing additional space aboard the boat—an invaluable commodity when you are on a world cruise and have to carry almost everything you will need. Many designs incorporate water tanks or fuel tanks in the keel. Additional storage space can be built into the keel for keeping food, storm gear, spare parts, or whatever. Finally, the keel permits the installation of an invaluable little invention—the bilge sump. No matter how water-tight your boat is, water *will* get inside—either from condensation, from rainwater, or from the ocean itself. And when it does, where do you think it's going to go when the boat heels over in a stiff breeze? Right. It will work its way up along the sides of the boat, sloshing into lockers and bunks, making the place miserable. With the bilge sump, however, that nightmare is avoided, and the foul-smelling water is trapped, to be eventually pumped out.

Finally, the hollow keel has the indispensable quality of strength. The fin keel can sheer off when struck by, say, a curious whale. But the hollow keel is an integral part of the hull; it may suffer dents or even penetration, but it will be unlikely to ever separate from the boat itself.

Everything considered, you are much better off with a hollow keel. The fin is cute and quick, but the hollow keel is safe and sane. Next decision: internal or external ballast?

Of the two types of hollow keel designs, each has its advocates. The external ballast keel has its ballast—a huge weight (usually lead) used to balance the boat—bolted from the outside to the bottom of the keel. It will be shaped so that it will conform to the contours of the hull (in effect, an almost indistinguishable extension of the keel). This type of design has two major benefits. First, there is less risk of damage if the vessel should happen to strike a rock or reef. Obviously, solid lead is less susceptible to damage than fiberglass or wood. Second, the ballast is slightly lower when attached externally, permitting a lower center of gravity and increased stability.

On the other hand, the internal ballast design avoids the use of keel bolts. The external lead weight must be bolted on to the hull; the bolts can corrode, or be severed in a collision, resulting in the ballast dropping from the keel. The sudden loss of your ballast can be, to say the least, a disconcerting experience: The boat will be extremely unstable and may capsize with little effort—never to right itself.

A second advantage to internal ballast is that the surface of the keel will have no seams or irregularities on its surface. The smoother face will mean less water resistance and a faster boat.

Mention should also be made of the variable draft keel. This is a design that uses a fin keel which can be retracted into the hull, either pivoting or drawing straight up—usually through the use of hydraulic or mechanical cranks. This can be a great advantage in shallow water sailing, such as in the Bahamas, but the structural and performance drawbacks for deep water cruising render the design generally less suitable than the fixed hollow keel.

Okay, now what about the rudder? Again, there are different designs offering different characteristics. In the heavy-duty, North Sea-type cruiser, the rudder may be a huge extension of a full-length keel; this offers great strength and stability, but fairly poor maneuverability. At the other extreme, the feather-light racer will have an isolated, razor-thin rudder extending down from the stern—quick but nervous, and most importantly there is little to prevent a floating log, a playful porpoise, or an unseen sand bar from twisting or shearing off the fragile, unprotected rudder.

The ideal cruising rudder falls somewhere between these extremes, and the available designs are endless. Each represents a compromise to some extent—speed versus stability, handling versus strength.

So there you are: more decisions. And advice in making those decisions is often no help at all; each sailor has his own particular favorites and prejudices. About the only way you can intelligently make such decisions is to be aware of the theoretical characteristics of each keel/rudder design, and then when you have narrowed it down to get out there and see how she sails!

There is one bit of advice that seems to hold true for keel and rudder configurations, as it does for anything else in cruising boats: avoid extremes. Obviously, a flat-out racing fin will be miserable in a heavy blow. Less obviously, a lumbering barge of a bow-to-stern keel designed to plow through typhoons can be equally unsuitable to life afloat. An example of this rule of moderation is found in the increasing popularity of the half-keel-and-skeg design, using a hollow keel dropping gradually from just behind the bow and ending about two-thirds back; it resumes again toward the stern in a skeg configuration (a smaller keel or fin that balances the boat while giving protection to the attached rudder). While it doesn't offer the quickness of the fin or the strength of the full keel, it still manages to combine an acceptable degree of maneuverability, speed, strength, stability, and rudder protection all in one design.

Size and Internal Design

Let's face it. A good big boat is better than a good little boat. Now there are going to be a lot of seasoned salts out there who consider this sacrilege—wizened mariners who will point out that *Dove* was a 24-footer and that the Atlantic was recently crossed in a 10-foot sloop! Granted, but comfortably? Quickly? Safely? Given equal quality in design and construction, the larger boat will sail faster, in more comfort, and with a greater degree of safety than a smaller boat.

Theoretically speaking, speed is directly proportional to the boat's waterline (again, assuming similar design, construction, and abilities of skipper and crew). The amount of sail that a given boat can raise is another basic factor in a boat's speed—and a larger boat can raise more sail than a smaller one. So the bigger boat is going to get you there faster. You say you're in no hurry? Maybe not for the first few weeks, but then you will find that making a fast run is one of the thrills of sailing. Fatigue is reduced, navigation is improved, and interesting landfalls come all that much more quickly. And what about that gale that is due to hit in three hours, and here you are racing for a safe port just about three hours' sail away? Besides, how many skippers can ignore the challenge of fellow mariners nosing up to their stern?

One of the biggest mistakes of the novice cruiser is to ignore speed in his search for safety and comfort. As a result, he buys a double-ended barge with sails, almost unsinkable—but also no fun to sail as it wallows among the waves like a sick cow. The world cruiser doesn't want a tender egg-shell racing machine, but he doesn't want a tank either. Make no mistake: Speed is desirable in a boat, to the degree that comfort and safety have not been unduly sacrificed. In fact, you will generally find that a fast cruising boat is often safer and more comfortable at sea than a slower one.

The second benefit of a larger boat is comfort. This elementary concept requires a little explanation. Quite simply, a longer boat will probably have more beam, and therefore more cubic feet of living space. The larger boat will be more likely to accommodate such luxuries as a hot-water heater, a gimballed oven, pressurized water, a shower, and so on; of course, as you will eventually discover, the greatest luxury at sea is simplicity, and too many gizmos in the boat just means more things that can—and will—go wrong. Finally, a larger boat will *generally* have a more comfortable motion at sea; the smaller boat will tend to be knocked about more easily by wave action.

Of course, size is a factor of more than just the boat's length. A boat with a broader *beam* (width) can have greater available living space than a narrow-beamed boat of greater length. Older yachts tended to be narrow beamed, almost knife-like, on the theory that this increased speed in the water. However, modern yacht designs are refuting this belief, and most racing yachts today are fairly broad-beamed—offering speed *and* space.

Related to the question of beam is that of the vessel's *draft*, the depth of the boat's hull. Here, again, moderation is the key to nautical design. A boat of too-shallow draft will prove less stable in rough seas, will probably not "track" as well, may have a more uncomfortable motion, and will offer less interior space. Too much draft, however, can slow the boat down because of increased wetted surface, will cause the boat to maneuver sluggishly, and can restrict the type of cruising grounds available (much of the Bahamas' grounds, for example, are so shallow that only shallow-draft boats can cruise widely).

Now that the virtues of the large sailboat have been praised, some warnings. First, and most obviously, the big ones are going to cost a whole lot more than the little ones. As boats increase in length, they rise exponentially in price. If a 30-footer costs $30,000, then the 33-foot model will cost $40,000, and the big 40-foot version will go for $90,000. Second, there are good little boats and bad big boats; size is absolutely no indication of quality. I have been speaking of comparing different-sized boats of equal design and construction, but there is no question that a well-built 28-footer is much more seaworthy than a poorly designed 40-foot dream ship. A smaller boat can be safer, it can be faster, and, surprisingly, it can even be more spacious than a larger boat, if the design and construction are superior. Third warning: Don't get more boat than you can handle. Maybe Sir Francis Chichester can sail a 60-footer around the world single-handedly, but you had better stick to a 35-foot job—at least, for the first year. Automatic pilots, self-furling sails, power winch windlasses, computerized navigational aids—these all make sailing the big ones a breeze. But what happens if any of these break down? And rest assured that they will! A rule of thumb in shopping for your boat: Always assume that every fancy thingamajig aboard will fall apart at the worst possible time; then ask yourself if you could safely sail the boat anyway.

Cabin Layout

There is only one word to describe the cabin designs of ocean-cruising sailboats—ingenious. That so much can be packed into such a small area for use under such widely varying conditions is nothing less than a miracle of engineering and imagination. Try to picture an area the size of a small kitchen. Imagine trying to cram beds, ovens, refrigerators, toilets, showers, chairs, and couches into that area. Now add all the clothing, food, fuel, water, toiletries, books, and the hundreds of miscellaneous items that you would need for your family for a period of, say, six months. Next, pile in stacks of sails, anchors, ropes, chains, oil, grease, life vests, tools, radios, charts, navigational aids and spare parts that a boat requires. Now try to imagine you and your family living in this tiny room jammed with equipment and supplies for six months—comfortably. Well, it *can* be done.

The ideal modern sailboat's cabin layout is a model of efficiency. There is not an inch of space that is wasted, and most items serve two or more purposes; everything is compact and functional. Materials tend to be of the highest quality to withstand the ravages of sea air and rough treatment. Accordingly, they run to the higher price tags.

Let's take a look at the basic types of floor plans used in the cruising sailboat. We will assume that that you are interested in a medium-sized cruiser, in the 33-foot range. To begin with, almost all cabin layouts in this size are going to have a similar basic floor plan: a small stateroom in the bow, possibly sealed off by a swinging or sliding door, and a main cabin, called a *salon*. The most common deviation from this is the recently popular aft cabin arrangement, where a third area is located in the stern, behind a midships cockpit; although this offers more privacy, it can also serve to reduce an already small boat into claustrophobic segments.

Most boats in this range will also have somewhat similar sleeping arrangements, usually accommodating six people. Two forward berths will be located in the forward cabin (in fact, they will fill it); two *quarter berths* will be arranged along the aft sides of the cabin, often underneath the cockpit; and a double berth will be found in the salon, usually convertible from a dinette arrangement. If there is an aft cabin, the quarter berths will be replaced by another double berth. Additionally, there may be hammock or transom extension berths that fold or slide out from the salon's *bulkheads* (walls).

The *head* (toilet) is usually enclosed in a closet-like room, located between the forward cabin and the salon; across from it, to balance the floor plan, will usually be a *hanging locker* (closet). Often, the enclosed head area will be rigged to be self-draining so that a hand-held or mounted shower can be used.

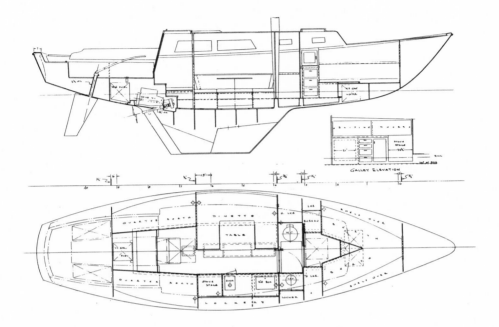

The cabin design of a midsized light cruiser, the fast and proven Cal 34.

The *galley* (kitchen) will normally be located in one of two places: (1) amidships, opposite the dinette, or (2) in the aft part of the salon next to the *companionway* (stairway/ladder leading up to the cockpit). There are some real benefits to having the galley next to the open air of the companionway. When you are down below in a heeled and pitching boat, peeling onions and frying bacon, the fresh air is more than welcome. Also, it's easier to wash dishes and pans near the companionway area. And, finally, the safety factor cannot be ignored: Fire from a kerosene or alcohol burner can be more easily reached in this area.

The remaining areas of the boat will be given over primarily to storage space: sections under the *sole* (floor); lockers; drawers; *lazarettes* (lockers under the cockpit seats); and shelving. Of course, room must be allotted for the auxiliary engine—most often, underneath or aft of the companionway.

A word about the cockpit. The tendency of novice sailors is to want a boat with the maximum cabin space for the boat's length, leaving relatively little space for the cockpit. After all, the cockpit is merely an open space in the stern; if there is room enough to sit and

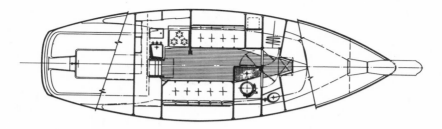

112

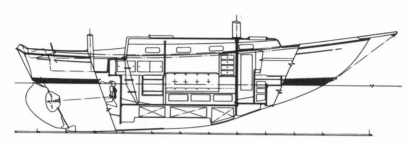

Top: The typically efficient cabin plan of a cruiser—here, of Allied's Seaward II 32. Above: The main cabin of the Seaward II 32, looking aft—neat, spacious, well planned.

steer, nothing more is needed. This is a mistake, as old salts well know. The cockpit is much more than just a place to steer from; it is where the cruising sailor will spend at least two-thirds of his life afloat. The skipper and crew will spend most of the daylight hours in the cockpit, going below only to cook or use the head; even at night, someone has to stand watch. And in warm climates, the cockpit quickly becomes the dining area and scene of makeshift bunks. The wise boat owner, therefore, will not minimize the importance of this critical area. At the same time, it must be recognized that an oversized cockpit, particularly a deep one, can represent a potential hazard. In rough seas, particularly following seas, the cockpit may be filled with water. Even a supposedly "self-draining" cockpit can take on more ocean than can quickly drain, and if there is enough water aboard (i.e., a large enough capacity in the cockpit), the boat may sink.

This, then, is the basic layout. Most proven cruisers in the mid-size market will reflect some variation of this design. Size, of course, will be a factor, and the larger the boat, the more options become available. As you get into the 40-footers—we're talking big money now—a comfortable tri-cabin layout becomes a real possibility, and two heads become minimum standard equipment. Conversely, the 26-footer will be a Spartan version of its big brothers—but still with the same basic forward berth-head-dinette/double berth-galley-quarter berth arrangement. But fair warning: Although the 26-footer will be correctly advertised as sleeping six, don't think that six people can comfortably live in an area that restricted for any real length of time!

113

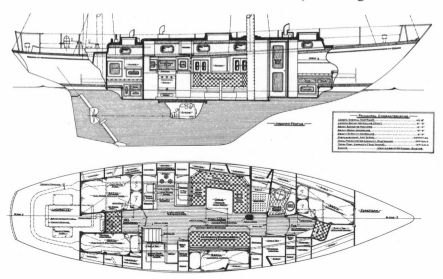

The cabin plan of a large cruising sailboat—the Mason 43.

There are certain variables in any cabin design that should be carefully considered, variables that can have a drastic effect on the comfort and morale of the boat's crew: ventilation, insulation, drainage, and lighting. Any cabin should be designed with an efficient system of fresh air ventilation, allowing the free flow of air through the entire cabin. This will help prevent mildew and rot in remote corners of the boat, and, perhaps more importantly, will make life bearable in the hot and humid climates of the tropics. Insulation is also important: It can inhibit condensation, dampen external sound, and moderate the internal temperature in hot or cold climates. Next, a good drainage system is critical. Water *will* get inside the boat—rainwater, salt water, dish water, shower water, etc. There should be a method for efficiently channeling this water into a central area, such as a sump, and then disposing of it by pumping out through the hull with an automatic or manual bilge pump. Without such a system, the cabin will quickly degenerate into a damp and foul-smelling place. Finally, the boat should have sufficient portholes and hatches to permit sunlight to enter the cabin. Without this, your new home can be a pretty dark and gloomy place.

To a certain degree, a boat's cabin layout is dictated by space and the realities of life at sea. But to a much greater extent than with basic boat design—hull shape, keel and rudder configuration, rigging, etc.—a boat's cabin layout can reflect the personal tastes of its skipper without an undue effect on safety and performance. Inside the cabin, comfort should be the primary consideration—comfort, and the pride of having an attractive and efficiently designed seagoing home.

Basic Equipment

In shopping for your new home, keep in mind that certain basic equipment will be necessary to your new life at sea. Most of that equipment will cost an arm and a leg to buy new, so if the boat you've got your eye on already has it, so much the better. Just make sure it's the right kind of equipment, and it's in good working condition.

The most expensive near-necessity is an auxiliary engine. All but the purest of cruising sailors recognize that there are times when sailpower is just not enough, and the back-up of a reliable engine can be mighty convenient if not an outright lifesaver. Consider trying to tack your 34-foot full-keel cruiser through a crowded anchorage in gusting winds; not a pleasant experience—and likely to end up in dented hulls and bruised feelings. And what do you do when your family has been frying under the blazing tropical sun for ten days with not a breath of wind to move the boat an inch? That is a common occurrence in the doldrum belt. Or what about getting caught near a rocky shore in a heavy blow, and the boat won't sail high enough to windward to work herself away? Or the sail rips? Or the mast goes?

No question about it: You should have an auxiliary engine. But what kind? If the boat is small enough, an outboard may suffice. If you've got a 26-footer, a 9-horsepower Johnson should do the job. But keep in mind the drawbacks of the outboard: It must be mounted or stored, it is relatively unreliable, and it requires a supply of highly explosive gasoline.

Any boat over 26 feet—and this will include 95 percent of world cruisers—should be equipped with an inboard engine. By *inboard* is meant that the engine is mounted permanently inside the boat—usually under the cockpit or companionway—and is linked to an external propeller by a shaft. It will be more expensive, but it is also more convenient, easier to steer, more powerful, safer, and more reliable.

Gas or diesel? Again, no contest: If you can afford the extra bucks, diesel is vastly superior to gas at sea. First, safety (*always* a paramount consideration in the middle of an ocean): Diesel is simply much less combustible than gasoline. Second, reliability: That diesel engine is going to start right up just about every time (and failing to start in a critical situation can spell doom for you and your boat). Third, economics: Diesel fuel is cheaper and the engine, though more expensive initially, will require fewer repairs. And finally, aesthetics: Ever compare the smell of gasoline with that of diesel?

So what you want in your dream home is an inboard diesel engine. Now, what about the tanks to hold the fuel? If the boat you are looking at doesn't have at least thirty-gallon tanks mounted somewhere inside the hull—usually in the hollow keel, along the bilges, or in the aft section of the lazarettes—then you are going to have to pay a whole lot of money to have them installed. Same goes with water tanks—although these should be in the 50–100 gallon range. A final note: Make sure the tanks are properly lined, are not corroding anywhere, and are mounted in an area designed to have minimal effect on the boat's weight balance.

Next: anchors and line. There should be at least two anchors, with the larger one tested sufficient to hold your boat in a good blow. The remaining anchor is your "lunch hook"—a lighter, more easily managed anchor for dropping over the side in calm, temporary anchorages. As to design, there is considerable controversy over the relative merits of mushroom versus plow, Danforth versus Northill, etc. Chances are you will find Danforths on your boat, and they are good, all-around anchors.

Along with the anchors, your future home should have plenty of anchor line and chain. Keeping in mind that an anchor line should be at least six times longer than the depth of the anchorage—more in rough conditions—you should have aboard at least 200 feet of line, together with twenty or thirty feet of chain. And that is in addition to the lighter line and chain for your back-up "lunch hook."

Next, you should be looking at the steering arrangement on the boat. Is it tiller or wheel? Each has its advantages. The tiller is cheaper and, being simpler, has less that can go wrong and is more easily repaired or jury-rigged. The wheel is easier to operate, requires less physical exertion, and is conceptually more logical (a left turn on a tiller results in a right turn of the boat, while wheel steering is the same as for a car).

The availability of a self-steering mechanism should also be considered. Keep in mind that handling the helm can be a very boring and tiring job; steering for twenty-four hours a day on a three-week passage can become downright tedious. Fortunately, there are devices that permit you to set a course and then get on with more important tasks—like taking a nap. These self-steering mechanisms are basically of two types: electronic auto-pilots and mechanical wind vanes.

The electronic gizmos work on the tiller or wheel to keep the boat on a set course, transmitting deviations from an internal compass to an electro-servo unit that continually corrects to the desired course. These are nice but expensive. However, the greatest drawback is the energy factor: They will suck about two to five amps an hour, and this can prove a big drain on your limited battery capacity at sea.

The wind vanes are preferable for long distance cruising. Basically, they translate changes in wind direction to servo or mechanical units which then correct the course through an auxiliary rudder or by direct action on the tiller or wheel. There are other variations, but most of them share the benefits of simplicity of operation (again, simplicity at sea means less that can go wrong) and lack of any energy drain.

The next thing you are going to want to look for is a sail inventory. Those two or three sails up there are not going to be enough. At the very least, you will need a couple of extra jib-type sails—preferably, a small, tough storm jib, and a big, lightweight "130" or "150" for light winds. For safety's sake, you should also have a back-up working jib, main, and mizzen. And don't forget to check the condition of the sails.

A real handy item—a necessity, really—is a dinghy. Whether of wood or fiberglass, or made out of tough rubber or synthetics like the Avon or Zodiac, the little rowboat will prove invaluable to you. Did you ever stop to think how you are going to get to shore once you are anchored in the middle of a harbor?

Check out the electrical power system. Make sure there are plenty of batteries—and in good condition. Of course, it goes without saying that the wiring, like the plumbing and joinder work, should be carefully inspected by a reputable marine surveyor (more on this in Chapter 11). If the boat has a generator, fine—but it is not a necessity and represents one more complex piece of equipment that can be a source of trouble. With ample battery capacity and moderate discipline in energy use, a cheap battery charger for use when dockside should be enough.

Of course, you are going to want a stove and, possibly, an oven. Make darned sure the stove/oven unit is gimballed and free-swinging laterally. Rare will be the time when you will be able to cook on a nice, calm sea; when the boat is rolling like a drunken sailor, it's helpful to be able to work on a stove-top that remains relatively level. Flying spaghetti can be really messy.

The stove/oven will burn either alcohol, LP (liquid petroleum), or kerosene. Alcohol is the most common because it is the safest: It will not explode and is less combustible than the other fuels. It is also the cleanest smelling. On the minus side, alcohol can be a son-of-a-gun to get started, and the fuel is expensive and sometimes hard to find. Kerosene is less popular today and has a slight odor, but it produces a hotter flame, is easier to work with, and is more readily found in remote cruising areas. Bottled LP-gas is convenient and efficient, but it is also potentially dangerous: Gas that leaks from the system, being heavier than air, will settle in the bilges, until a spark from the electrical system blows the boat into the heavens. Electrical stoves should be avoided, unless you plan on doing your cruising tied up to a yacht club dock.

The list of equipment could go on and on. But as for necessary gear, we will just mention navigational aids: a top quality corrected and mounted compass; a fathometer (depth-sounder); a knotmeter (the boat's speedometer); a good sextant of the Plath type; and a chronometer (an accurate clock for use in celestial navigation).

You are going to need much of this stuff—no two ways about it. So if you can find a boat with most of it already aboard—and many used blue-water sailboats are sold fully equipped—then there is that much more money left for cruising.

Okay. So now you are beginning to get a pretty good idea of just what you want in a cruising boat. But does such a boat exist? How much does it cost? Where do I find it?

In the next chapter, I will look at a wide range of modern cruising sailboats—from a Spartan 20-footer to a 42-foot seagoing mansion. We will look over the current new offerings, then consider some of the better used models on the market—and where those markets are. Finally, for those on a tight budget, we will even check out some classic old wooden boats that sell for peanuts but sail like the tough, proven veterans that they are.

10

A Look at the Market

In the long run, men hit only what they aim at. Therefore, though they should fail immediately, they had better aim at something high.

You have done some chartering or weekend sailing, you have read about cruising needs and basic sailboat design, and now you are ready to go shopping for your own boat. It's time to take a closer look at what is available out there.

Very roughly, there are three basic kinds of suitable cruising vessels, and three ways to buy them. You can buy a heavy-displacement boat designed specifically for blue-water cruising; you can look for a more conventional sailboat, of medium displacement; or you can get yourself a modern, lighter-displacement greyhound. And you can buy the boat brand new; you can shop for a used boat; or you can build it yourself, either from scratch or from a bare-hull kit.

Before you automatically jump into one category, however, you should be aware of the relative advantages and disadvantages involved. Some mention has been made in the previous chapter of the merits of different aspects of sailboat design, but a few general observations are in order. The heavy displacement boats, such as the recent wave of double-ended designs, are solid, roomy, and built to take on a hurricane. They have plenty of living space below decks, and they will track fairly easily; they will plow through rough seas and put dents in coral heads. On the other hand, too many of them are deadly slow; their great bulk causes them to wallow in anything less than a minor gale. While they will track well, their maneuverability is often roughly that of a railroad train. And, perhaps most importantly, they can be a son-of-a-gun to sail to windward. What good is toughness if the boat will not go where you want it to?

The understandable attitude of the novice cruiser is to search for a vessel that is built like a Sherman tank. His paramount concern is safety, and to the individual who is not thoroughly familiar with sailing and cruising, this means heavy displacement, full lead keels, and equipment designed for a pocket battleship. Unfortunately, safety is not just a factor of bulk; a lighter, quicker sailboat can be much safer. Any given reef or storm, if big enough, will sink a cruising boat no matter what the design. On the other hand, that reef or storm can be avoided more easily with a fast boat: The storm can be outrun; the reef can be avoided by tacking hard to windward. Which is "safer" in city traffic—a Mack truck or a sports car?

On the other hand, the modern fiberglass whippets can prove too tender for blue-water voyages. Referred to as "floating Clorox bottles" by many of the cruising fraternity, they offer all the speed, maneuverability, and ease of handling that could reasonably be desired. Yet all but the best designed of them will be knocked around unmercifully by heavy seas; a good storm could seriously damage or even sink one of these craft designed for weekend racing or cruising.

The basic problem of such boats—and the majority of sailboats produced today are of this type—is that they are designed with the wrong considerations in mind. First, many are designed to "beat the ratings": The boat is purposely planned not for efficiency but to take advantage of quirks in the esoteric racing handicap rules. Second, most of these boats are built strictly for racing, daysailing, or weekend gunkholing; they are simply not intended for taking on a raging gale. Third, economy is a prime consideration in both design and construction: The boat may well be built with as cheap materials and labor as possible. And the stresses of blue-water cruising will quickly uncover cheap gear or shoddy worksmanship.

Of course, the seaworthiness of a boat is not going to be the only consideration in your coming days of shopping for your future home. Price is going to be a determinative factor. You may find the ideal boat for your plans—ruggedly built and designed for fast, windward performance—but if it costs $100,000, you keep looking. Here we should consider the merits of buying new and buying used. As has been touched on briefly in previous chapters, the new boat is obviously going to cost more. It is always nice to be able to buy your boat right off the assembly line, unsoiled by anyone else, and with everything in (theoretically) perfect working order. But the price is high. And not just because of the purchase price: A brand-new $50,000 sailboat can easily require another $10,000 of equipment to make her suitable for extended cruising. Such items as depth finders, wind vanes, dinghies, and spare sails do not come cheaply.

A used boat, on the other hand, is usually going to come fairly well equipped—at least with the gear normally needed for weekend sailing. And if the boat is a blue-water design, there is a good chance it will be loaded with all the goodies you could want for a circumnavigation—thus saving you thousands of dollars in additional expenses. It is not uncommon to come across boats put on the market by individuals who have finished their cruising days, or—more sadly— who have learned too late that the cruising lifestyle is not for them. Every yacht broker can tell you stories of couples who have planned their cruise for years, purchased a fine vessel, elaborately equipped it with the best, and then have taken off on their dream—only to return in a few days, green with seasickness and screaming at each other, and put the boat up for sale.

Buying used has another fringe benefit. A new boat requires a "breaking in" period—a time for ironing out all the kinks. Much more so than with a car, a boat is going to take some time and work to seal all the leaks, to get the stove working properly, to isolate electrical problems. And this can take months. A used boat, presumably, has these bugs already ironed out: Once necessary repairs (if any) are made, it should be ready to go.

Used boats are usually cheaper. But, of course, they can also be more expensive. Some boats simply appreciate in value as they get older because of their quality; the Hinckley is an example. Others are overpriced by unrealistic sellers. And still others will seem a bargain but end up costing you more in repairs and replacements than it would have buying new. Common sense—that single indispensable quality of a cruising sailor—should guide you in your shopping the used boat market. Common sense, that is, *and* a good surveyor (more about that in the next chapter).

Buying a used boat is considerably more involved than buying a used car or house. The boat is simply more complex, and the risks are higher. The buyer, then, should be infinitely more careful in inspecting a used sailboat than he would be for a car or house. Lacking expertise, you must ask around and get the best—even if most expensive—marine surveyor available who specializes in the type of boat you are looking for.

One way to be fairly assured that the boat is solidly built is to look for a "Lloyd's 100 A1" rating. Lloyd's Register of Shipping is an organization which sets standards for the construction of all kinds of boats and ships; if the vessel is built in accordance with their demanding requirements—and very few are—then the company issues a "100 A1" certificate. Such a rating does not mean the boat has not suffered from poor maintenance or damage, of course, but it does indicate that it was built properly to begin with.

Nor does the fact that the boat is without a Lloyd's certificate mean the construction was substandard. Many boats are simply built without asking for a Lloyd's inspection. However, you can compare the construction specifications of the yacht's builder (if available) with those required by Lloyd's. Your surveyor should have access to Lloyd's specifications and can tell you if the boat complies. Or write Lloyd's Register Printing House, Manor Crawley, West Sussex, RH 10 2QN, England, and advise them what type of boat you want information about—fiberglass, wood, or whatever. If you also want their specifications on electrical circuitry, plumbing, etc., request them also. The cost is about five pounds sterling for the construction specs, ten pounds for a complete set of machinery specs, which include circuitry, propeller shafts, and the rest.

You will want to "sea trial" the boat before you buy it. That is, you and the owner should sail for a day or two so that you get the feel for how the boat handles. All the inspections in the world will not necessarily disclose the fact that the boat sails like a barge.

There is an even less expensive alternative than buying used—building your own boat. If you are handy with your hands, and time is not a consideration, you can save a lot of money by simply building the vessel of your dreams. And saving money is not the only benefit: There is no better way to know your boat than to put her together with your own hands. This intimate knowledge is invaluable during emergencies, as well as for routine maintenance and repairs. Also, constructing your own boat guarantees that everything aboard is going to be as you want it. No boat on the market is going to mirror your needs or desires in every detail; if you build it yourself, it will.

There are drawbacks, however; time is the principal one. The backyard construction of a 35-foot cruising vessel can take years to complete. Space may be another problem: Do you have the area needed for the boat, tools, and equipment? And costs can be deceptive. You can actually end up spending more money building your own boat than you would if you had bought a comparable vessel from a manufacturer—particularly if you have to contract out when it comes to such skills as wiring, cabinetwork, plumbing, or rigging. And

121

remember that your costs for materials can be much higher than those of manufacturers; it has been estimated that the cost of totally replacing all the parts of a new yacht, with labor, would be almost double the new price of the yacht.

A final drawback is hull construction. Quite simply, the average mechanically skilled do-it-yourselfer does not have the equipment or ability to construct a good fiberglass hull. Even wood hulls are very difficult to build correctly; steel is almost impossible. Which leaves ferrocement, the hull material employed by most backyarders today. Yet there is another possibility: the kit boat. Some manufacturers— Westsail is the most notable, having made kit-boat cruisers popular— offer bare hulls for sale. A few manufacturers will even offer their boats in various stages of completion: bare hull; hull and deck; hull, deck, and rigging; or complete except for cabinetwork. The savings, of course, decrease as the boat is purchased more complete.

A kit boat (the Mariner 32) in the final stages of completion by its owner.

Now that you know of the availability of kit boats, incidentally, you should be on guard during your shopping for a used boat. The Westsail or Mariner or whatever you are looking at may have, in reality, been put together by the owner. Many of these kit boats are constructed as solidly and skillfully as they would have been at the factory, but many also reflect the ignorance or clumsiness of their builders. When considering a used boat, try to find out if it was built by the owner—either from scratch or from a kit. Then try to find out a little about the owner, before your surveyor gives the boat a particularly close look.

A look now at boats available on today's market. Some warnings, however. First, the prices are for used boats as of 1981; assuming continued inflation, you can expect the prices to be accordingly higher by the time you read this, or possibly lower if the model is discontinued, depreciates generally, or falls out of fashion. Second, the prices are very general and can vary widely according to the age and condition of the boat, location, current tastes and fads in boats, equipment, and "condition" of the owner. Third, the manufacturers and models listed are far from exhaustive. The boats discussed hereafter represent only a few of the more common suitable models. Finally, the selection will undoubtedly draw disagreement as it necessarily reflects the opinions of the author alone.

There have been very few steel, aluminum, or ferrocement yachts made in quantity, and very few wood boats made any more. Consequently, we will be looking at relatively recent fiberglass designs, with later analysis of the possibilities of older boats.

Heavy-displacement cruisers. There have been a number of high-quality boats built in recent years of the heavy, rough-weather type. These have been influenced often by the rugged North Sea vessels and the famous Tahiti ketch, as well as by nautical architect Robert Perry's drawing board. They are usually double-ended, with a rounded or pointed stern, and are heavily constructed, broad of beam, with a trunk cabin and a full keel. They are generally solid, comfortable boats, but with relatively poor sailing performance to windward or in lighter airs. And they are expensive—partly because of quality, partly because few of them are more than six or seven years old, and partly because they are in fashion.

You will find a large number of these types of boats on the market today, reflecting a recent trend toward boats designed specifically for blue-water cruising. Usually, the boat will be heavily stocked with cruising equipment, and as a result you may find a good buy.

Probably the prime mover in the recent trend toward this type of boat was the Westsail Corporation, with their 32- and 42-foot models. There are a lot of these boats on the market today—many of them built from kits, however. A good Westsail 32 will run in price from around $45,000 to $60,000; the 42-footer or 43-footer will go for about double that. The newer Westsail 28 will cost around $40—45,000.

The Rolls-Royce niche in this category has got to be shared by Valiant and Hans Christian. Both build beautiful state-of-the-art world cruisers, but the price tags reflect it. A Valiant 40 will go for about $140,000, with a Hans Christian 38 hitting the $90,000 range. Lovely boats, if you can afford them.

Some other well-built models in this category are the Alajuela 38 (around $90,000), the Ingrid 38 ($85,000), the Rafiki 37 ($75—85,000), the Tayana 37 ($70,000 or so), and the Crealock 36 ($70,000).

Stepping down a bit in size, there is the Alajuela 33 ($70,000), Hans Christian 34 ($70,000), Mariah 31 ($60,000), Baba 30 ($50—60,000), Nor'Sea 27 ($45,000), and Pacific Seacraft 25 ($20,000).

Expensive.

Conventional middle-displacement boats. In this category are found a wide variety of boats constructed solidly but along more traditional lines. Generally, they represent a compromise between safety and performance: They aren't floating fortresses like the Westsail or Hans Christian, and they won't win many races in light winds against the formula greyhounds. But they are fairly fast (particularly when the wind picks up), maneuverable, comfortable, and safe. Very generally, they tend to be built with transom sterns and keels that reflect a compromise between the sluggish full keel and the tender fin keel. They are excellent cruisers, and cost considerably less than the heavy displacement jobs.

The Cadillac in this group has got to be the Hinckley. Made by an old-line outfit in New England, the Hinckley is a beautiful example of Yankee shipbuilding skill—a fast but seaworthy yacht. And, of course, the price tag reflects it: A Hinckley Pilot 35 model can run used anywhere from $55,000 to $75,000.

Perhaps next in line is the excellent Japanese-built Fuji. The 35-footer will cost about $65,000, while the 32-foot version can be had for somewhere in the vicinity of $55,000. Some of the other good boats in this category include: the Cheoy Lee 35 ($40,000 plus or minus) and 30 ($30,000); the Mariner 31 or 32 ($30,000); the Alberg 35 ($35,000), 30 ($23,000), and 27 ($16,000); the Cape Dory line, including the 30 ($35,000) and 28 ($28,000); and the Morgan 33 ($35–40,000) and 30 ($30,000).

Special mention should be made of two unusual boats in this category. The Freedom is a new design, with free-standing graphite masts—i.e., without shrouds or stays. Initial indications are that the design works well and, should time treat it favorably, will be an excellent choice. The boats are too new to have used prices at this time, however. The Flicka is another interesting design, an excellent 20-foot cruiser! Built by Pacific Seacraft, the vessel is solid, eminently liveable, surprisingly fast, and capable of world cruises. One can be obtained used for around $15,000.

Conventional middle-light-displacement boats. These welterweights are closely related to the previous category, and in some cases indistinguishable; admittedly, these classifications are the author's and are subject to argument. Generally, however, these boats

The surprisingly spacious interior of the Flicka 20-foot minicruiser.

are a bit lighter—and, thus, a bit faster, a bit more maneuverable, and a bit more tender. Often modified racing designs, they are performance boats that are capable of blue-water cruising. They represent by far the most prevalent of cruising vessels, as they are most often used for local pleasure cruising. And they are the least expensive of fiberglass boats because of their lower initial cost and their numbers.

The Pearson line of boats is an example of the excellent cruising designs available in this group. Combining speed, windward ability, comfort, and general seakindliness, the Pearson yachts are excellent choices. The modern 323 and 365 are beautiful boats, but not yet widely available on the used market. A used 35-footer can be had for $45–50,000, but most interesting perhaps are their older, small cruisers—the 32-foot Vanguard ($30,000), the 28-foot Triton ($15,000), and the 26-foot Ariel ($12,000).

The Cal boats are another good line of fast cruisers. The old Cal 40 was a consistent winner of ocean races and makes a fine cruiser at around $40,000 to $50,000. The aging Cal 34 is another good choice, selling at about $35,000. Two smaller models in their older line suitable for cruising are the 29 ($25,000) and 27 ($17,000 or so).

Tartan makes some good boats, including the 33-footer at around $35,000 and the 30-foot model at $30,000. The Ericson 35 is an outstanding cruising boat, combining proven performance and seaworthiness; at $35,000 to $45,000, they are good buys. Many of the older Columbias, Islanders, Coronados, and Lapworths are also worth taking a close look at. By way of illustrative prices, the Columbia 29 will cost around $17,000, the Columbia 34 about $35,000, the Islander 37 runs $40,000, the Islander 32 for $25,000 for the older version, the Coronado 30 goes for somewhere around $22,000, and the Lapworth-Cal 30 costs about $22,000 (it was in a 24-foot Lapworth that Robin Lee Graham sailed around the world in his teens).

Wood. Last, but certainly not least, consider the wood boat. Consider it very seriously, for it represents a real value in today's boat market. There are drawbacks to wood, just as there are benefits, and these have been discussed in the previous chapter. But there is absolutely nothing inherently wrong with wood for cruising. There have been more circumnavigations in wooden yachts than in all others combined. Yet the price of a wood vessel of equivalent size, quality, and condition can be as little as half that of its fiberglass counterpart.

The reasons for this are simple: Wood boats are usually older, require more maintenance, and, most importantly, are simply "out of style." The average sailor today wants the latest of everything in his boat, and wood is just old-fashioned. Also, there is a constant fear of wood rot or infestation by worms; these can be prevented.

So if you are truly cost-conscious, take a good look at some wood sailboats. You will have to be more careful in inspecting the condition of the hull and decks, but a wood boat in good condition can be a heck of a buy.

The more modern, good quality wood boats are represented by Kettenburg. These big beauties run in price from as little as $9,000 for their 32-footer, to $25,000 for the 38-foot model, and on up to the 40-footer at $40,000—a fine boat. Mason made a good 38-footer at $40,000 which is worth looking at, if you can find one.

And then there are the husky double-enders, forerunners of the presently popular heavy-displacement cruisers. Most of these were not models from a boat manufacturer, but were built either by the owner or by a shipyard to order. The Tahiti ketch is the best known of these—a tough, lumbering boat designed to sail right through an island. A 30-foot Tahiti ketch will run anywhere from $15,000 to $25,000. The Hanna ketch is a similar design, and these massive 33- and 34-foot boats have recently appreciated in cost up to around $40,000, due to the popularity of the Valiants, Westsails, and their kind.

Three other designs are worth mentioning: Atkins, Alden, and Angleman—all fine cruisers. The Alden 34 goes for around $35,000;

Top row, left: The wooden 26-foot International Folkboat, a proven ocean-crosser at $8,000. Top, right: This homely little one-of-a-kind wooden boat is solid, seaworthy—and on the market for $10,000. Second row, left: Another ugly-but-seaworthy wooden cruiser that can be bought for $12,000. Second, right: The Pearson 28-foot Triton, an excellent older fiberglass cruiser that can be had for around $15,000. Third row, left: Veteran of a circumnavigation, this wooden 30-footer is for sale at $22,000. Third, right: A solidly built double-ended wooden ketch on the market for $25,000. Bottom row, left: A beautiful wooden 35-foot ketch for sale at $28,000. Bottom, right: The Ericson 35—a fast, proven cruiser that can be bought used for $35,000.

the Atkins 32 runs closer to $20,000; and the Angleman 36 will cost you in the neighborhood of $35,000 to $40,000.

Many of the fiberglass boat makers have also made good wooden boats in the past. These include the Lapworth 36 (about $35,000) and the Cheoy Lee 35 ($38,000).

Special mention should be made of the International Folkboat for those with particularly thin pocketbooks and Spartan requirements. These slender little wood boats have sailed all over the world and have repeatedly proven themselves. They are tight for space, but a single-hander could get a boat ready for blue-water sailing for a song: around $7,000 or $8,000 used for either the 25- or 26-foot design.

Finally, it should be noted that wooden boats come in an endless variety of designs. They are remnants of an age when boats were not popped off the assembly line by the dozens, but were carefully handcrafted one at a time. As a result, it is difficult to list or categorize when you are discussing wood boats. There are literally hundreds of designs out there, many of them one-of-a-kind. Their lack of uniformity is not necessarily a reflection on their seaworthiness. Many of them are rotting disasters, but many are top-quality world cruisers. The fact that wood is not popular and that the design is not well known should not preclude you from taking a look; on the contrary, this will simply reduce the price of what may be an excellent boat. Listing sample prices of such boats would be pointless without knowing the boat. Suffice to say that there are good blue-water boats out there that will safely and comfortably carry you and your family anywhere—for as little as $10,000 or $20,000. All they require is a little more loving care than their more expensive fiberglass cousins.

11

Of Brokers, Bankers, and Surveyors

Through want of enterprise, men are where they are, buying and selling, and spending their lives like serfs.

All right. You have a pretty good idea of just what you are looking for out there in the boat market. Now it is just a question of how to go about finding it. And, having found it, how to determine the condition of the boat. Then, how to deal with the owner. Finally, assuming the vessel passes muster, there are the entangling matters of escrow, financing, insurance, registration, and taxes.

To begin with, let us assume that you are taking the economically wise course of looking for a used boat rather than a new one. And there are two ways to do this—with and without a yacht broker.

About yacht brokers. There are brokers, and then there are brokers. In other words, the yacht brokerage field is like any other—there are the good ones and the bad ones, the honest ones and those not so honest. Some of them are rank amateurs who will know less about boats than your next-door neighbor does; others will be transpac skippers or experienced circumnavigators. To last a few years, though, a broker is going to have to be fairly reputable, so look for brokers who have been around for awhile. And don't feel bashful about asking other sailors for recommendations; usually a few polite inquiries around the local marina will result in a list of names you can consider.

Now try to narrow this list down to brokers who deal in the price range in which you are interested, and who specialize in cruising sailboats. As you can tell from scanning the brokerage ads in the back of the yachting magazines, there are gold-plated brokerage houses that would not soil their white gloves with anything less than a $100,000 vessel. These people are simply not interested in your business and would not have the listings you would be interested in anyway. Look instead for the brokers who have the kinds of listings that fall within your category—blue-water cruisers, old wooden boats, or whatever. They are interested in your business, and they will know the market better than the broker whose main clientele consists of day sailors or racing fanatics.

Don't feel bound to just one broker, however. There is nothing legally or ethically to prevent you from visiting several brokers and seeing what they have to offer—both in the way of services and in boat listings. Most of them will have notebooks filled with pictures and specifications for their listed yachts; take a look at a few of these notebooks to get a good idea of what is available out there. The broker who ends up having the boat you want is the one with whom you will do business. It's like shopping for a house: You are not tied, as a buyer, to a particular broker. The seller, however, may be. If he has signed an "exclusive" with a broker, then only that broker will have the listing; other brokers may provide a buyer, but they will have to split the commission. A general listing, on the other hand, is like a real-estate multiple listing: All brokers are in on the deal, although the broker who listed the vessel will get a cut of the action. Obviously, then, a brokerage will advertise and promote an exclusive listing much more than they will a general listing. The result may be that the boats that are pushed at you initially will not necessarily be the ones that are most suited to your needs but will simply be the agency's exclusive listings. Keep that in mind before you jump at one of the first boats you see.

After you have looked at all the pretty pictures and misleading specifications in the broker's office, you will pick out three or four to visit. This is a good time to assess whether this broker is for you. Is he, for example, trying to sell you a boat that is higher in price than you have specified? If so, then this guy is interested in only one thing— getting a bigger commission. Is he trying to cover up his unfamiliarity with the particular boat you are looking at? Then he is being dishonest; an ethical broker will simply explain that he is not yet familiar with the vessel's history, condition, or performance characteristics.

So what do these brokers cost? That depends upon how you look at it. They do not cost you a thing directly. Their money comes from a commission that is paid by the seller—usually in the neighborhood of 6 to 10 percent of the purchase price. But it does not take much to figure that you may be paying that commission indirectly: If the seller wants $40,000 for his boat, he may put it on the market for $44,000 in order to be able to clear his price after the brokers take their cut. And many brokers will raise the price to, say, $49,000 on the theory that a buyer will insist on negotiating a lower price—or perhaps they'll raise the price simply to increase their commission.

Then why enlist a broker's services? Primarily because he offers such extensive lists of yachts to choose from, complete with photographs, history, specifications, and lists of equipment. You could spend the next year scouring the docks and probably not come up with the number of boats that fit your needs as you would by simply visiting a few brokerages. A good broker will see exactly what you are looking for and immediately zero in on just about every boat in the area that comes close—at least, every boat that has been listed with a broker.

A couple of other good reasons for using a broker: He has experience, and he can take care of the messy details. A good broker who specializes in cruising sailboats will probably be, or have been, a blue-water cruiser himself, and he can give you the benefit of his accumulated wisdom. He may suggest, for example, that you would be better off with a wind vane than with an electronic auto-pilot because of the battery drain at sea. Or he may be aware that a particular boat is a fine sailer but tends to pitch wildly in a rough sea. At the same time, the broker can guide your purchase of the boat through all the headaches of paperwork (do not, however, let the broker take care of the survey; many brokers will hire a surveyor who will go easy on the boat so as not to blow the deal).

This is not to say that you should not try to shop for your dream boat on your own. There is nothing that says that enlisting the services of a broker precludes you from trying to find a boat by yourself. Just be sure that the boat you do find is not one that was shown to you in the broker's office—or you may be paying his commission yourself.

How do you go about looking for a boat on your own? You start by scanning the advertisements in the boating magazines and in the classified section of the newspaper. This will give you a rough idea of what is generally available, and what the current asking prices are. Then follow up on the more interesting ads. Call the owners. Inquire about the age of the boat, general condition, type of equipment, how the boat has been used. Make an appointment to take a look at it; if possible, take a short sail with the owner.

Another way is simply to walk around the local marinas and do some browsing. Boats that are for sale will usually have a sign up—at least, if they are for sale by the owner. Often, you will stumble across exactly the boat you have been searching for. Take a look at the bulletin boards of the marinas, yacht clubs, and shopping markets in the area for ads posted by boat owners.

Yet another possibility is to visit a new boat dealer. Some of the dealerships in cruising sailboats will take older cruisers in trade, and they are usually anxious to unload these boats as soon as possible; they are not used boat dealers, and the "eyesore" is taking up a valuable slip.

Once you have located a boat that interests you, you should try to get an experienced hand to give it a closer look. Eventually, of course, you will want to have the vessel inspected closely by a surveyor, but for now the screening process demands an initial but thorough probing.

If you are going to rely upon your own observations, be aware initially that most boats up for sale are just not worth buying. The boat is being sold for a reason, and that reason may be that it would cost more to repair than it is worth. Any rotting hulk can be cosmetically patched up and painted over so as superficially to appear sound. And there are all too many buyers who, blinded by a dream, *want* desperately to believe the boat is in good condition.

The most critical thing to look for if the boat is wooden is *dry rot*. Dry rot is a common but particularly insidious problem in many wood boats. It is a fungus that grows in damp wood that has insufficient fresh air circulating; like most fungi, it will spread fairly quickly throughout the boat until, unchecked, the vessel disintegrates and heads for the bottom. If it is in advanced stages in the boat you are looking at, forget it.

Look for the beginnings of dry rot in those areas of the hull and deck that are most inaccessible, since this is where light and fresh air are least likely to reach. Check out the farthest corners of the bilge; pull up floorboards, open lockers, go into the engine area; inspect the frames and overhead/deck. When you find a suspicious place, stick a knife blade into the wood; if the blade goes in much over one-eighth of an inch, you probably have dry rot.

Of course, the presence of dry rot does not automatically mean the boat is a reject. If it is localized, you can yank out the infected wood and replace it with new lumber. If this can be done without extensive work, the boat may be a good buy: The asking price may plummet, as discovery of dry rot in a vessel is much like uncovering bubonic plague in the neighborhood.

Check the seams between the planks below the waterline (from inside). If the boat is out of the water and there is space between the boards, it will probably disappear once the boat is again in the water and the planks swell. If the boat is afloat and water is coming in through spaces, the seam may not be structurally sound, and even re-caulking will prove futile. Knock on the seam: If it has a hollow sound, then the inner, abutting edges may have been rotted or worn off.

The presence of *rust* is another thing to look for. To begin with, it is an indication of a skipper who does not maintain his vessel. If rust is present, then there will probably be other problems as well. Advanced rust can, of course, be serious, particularly if it is present in the hull fastenings.

Electrolysis is another weakness to check for. Electrolysis is the chemical reaction between underwater iron screws or fittings and nearby copper, bronze, or brass. The sails should be inspected for mildew as well as for tears at the stress points. The shrouds and stays must be checked for rust, particularly around the turnbuckles. And investigate the boat's engine, preferably by running it for a time underway at sea. Unusual vibration can mean a misaligned shaft, defective mountings, bent propeller, or any of a number of other things. The cooking system should be looked at for the presence of corrosion. Fuel and oil consumption should be noted.

A word about dealing with sellers. If he is the type of person who is telling you that there are two or three other guys seriously considering buying the boat, walk away from the deal. There are other boats—plenty of them—and this one is being sold by a high-pressure artist. If he has to resort to tactics like that, then he may well be anxious to unload the boat for a reason not apparent to you.

Keep in mind that you have the edge in these deals. Make an offer below the selling price. Most owners are in somewhat of a hurry to sell: The costs of slip fees, maintenance, marine insurance, and the boat mortgage are piling up. This eager seller may lose the deal by turning down your low-ball offer. You, on the other hand, are one of a small number of buyers in a market with plenty of sellers; there is no shortage of boats for you to look at elsewhere, and he knows it. More than likely, he will come back with a counteroffer, perhaps splitting the difference.

Any offer—whether made privately or through a broker—should always be made subject to sea trial and survey. The written agreement

133

should specifically state that the deal is off if for any reason you are dissatisfied with the results of either the sea trial or the survey.

What are a sea trial and a survey?

A *sea trial* is just what it sounds like—a test of the boat at sea. You, the owner, and probably your broker, will take the vessel out of the marina and sail her for a few hours—or a couple of days, if that is the arrangement you wish. This is your chance to see how the boat behaves in a following sea, hard to wind, and so on. Everything should be checked under working conditions at sea: the engine, head, stove, fathometer, self-steering gear, compass, radio, bilge pumps, sails, and running rigging. If possible, bring along someone who is particularly knowledgeable in cruising, or at least in sailing.

It should be mentioned that before putting the owner to the time and trouble of this test sail, you have tendered "offer money"— perhaps 10 percent of the agreed purchase price. This is held in escrow much as if you were buying a house. The primary conditions of escrow are completion of the sea trial to your satisfaction, a survey, and probably a quick inventory of the vessel's equipment. Once you have approved of the boat's performance in the sea trial, then the only thing left is the survey.

A *survey* is simply a detailed inspection of the boat—usually by an expert called, appropriately enough, a *surveyor*. The boat is hauled out of the water (you should absolutely insist on this) so that your surveyor can take a close look at the boat's bottom and pull a keel bolt or two out for inspection. The cost of this surveyor, as well as the boatyard's charges for the haul-out, must be borne by you. It can be expensive, with a surveyor charging perhaps a couple of hundred dollars, and the yard hitting you up for another hundred or so. And you must foot the bill, regardless of whether the deal goes through or not. But the survey is a critical step: It can uncover serious problems with the boat that you cannot. Don't even think of buying a boat that you are going to trust with your family's lives at sea without having it surveyed first.

Your surveyor will give you some initial impressions after he is finished (it may take him a couple of hours of snooping and probing), and he will follow this up with a detailed, written report. Your broker or the buyer, incidentally, may have a recent or not-so recent survey report on the boat, but you should insist on a new survey conducted by a surveyor of your own choosing.

The survey is, by the way, an excellent chance to become very familiar with your future home at sea. Some surveyors resent

A wooden sloop about to undergo a thorough out-of-the-water survey.

being accompanied during their inspection of the boat; try to find one that does not. Then, ask him to explain the various intricacies of the vessel's construction and equipment as he crawls in and out of it—with you following. It's a great way to learn about the guts of the boat, and the information is almost guaranteed to come in handy on more than one critical occasion in future years at sea.

Another thing to consider is scraping and painting the boat while she is hauled out. If the surveyor tells you that the report will be favorable, and you are fairly sure that the deal will go though, why not scrape and paint the hull? The only cost is for paint and the haul-out charge—and you've already paid the haul-out charge. The boatyard may ask for a few bucks more for a day or two of space rental.

The surveyor's report (the survey) will contain a complete analysis of the boat's condition: the hull, rigging, electrical system, and permanent equipment all will be gone over, and his opinions as to their condition expressed. His limitations should, however, be understood. First, he cannot tell you how the boat will perform at sea; that is the purpose of the sea trial. Second, many surveyors will not go up the mast; the condition of the upper mast and rigging is open to question, therefore, although the lower rigging and mast should be an indication. Third, if the hull is of fiberglass, the surveyor cannot judge its basic integrity. He can interpret surface flaws, such as cracks, voids, or crazing, but the ultimate integrity will be an unknown. He may, however, be able to offer information concerning his knowledge of the practices employed by the boat's builder.

A negative survey is not necessarily the end of the deal. Certainly, if there are serious problems, you should walk away from the deal. But if the problems are minor or remediable, you should be able to get the buyer to lower the price enough to cover the costs of the repairs—and possibly more, considering the time you will have to spend obtaining the repairs.

Where do you get a surveyor?

As with brokers, there are good surveyors and bad surveyors. These men are usually very experienced in their fields; many are retired merchant marine skippers with vast stores of knowledge. They can be found in telephone and marine directories or by asking around at marine insurance firms or boatyards. Get a few opinions before retaining a surveyor. Make sure he has a reputation concerning cruising sailboats; some surveyors handle ships or power boats almost exclusively. And make darned sure he has no connection with your broker.

Finally, some mention of paperwork common to boat purchases.

Financing. As has been mentioned earlier in this book, if you are seeking a better way of life cruising the oceans of the world, then leave the entanglements of city life behind: Forget financing. Pay cash. The interest rates are deadly; the payments will be a heavy yoke around your neck wherever you sail so that you can never really feel completely free; and the bank or other lending institution will insist on your carrying marine insurance—if they "permit" you to sail "their" boat into distant waters at all.

It is another matter, of course, if you are following the 1-Year Plan, i.e., financing the boat while you live aboard, with the intention of paying off the mortgage or loan before leaving. In such a case, shop around for the best interest rates, making sure the loan agreement contains no prepayment penalty clause. Many banks have special boat-loan departments. And there are lending institutions that specialize in boat loans; these can be found in yachting magazines and at boat shows. But do not advise the lender that you are planning to take off for the high seas, leaving the world behind; bankers are conservative people, and they get very nervous.

Insurance. Again, as mentioned elsewhere, forget it! Insurance is a big rip-off. You will have to carry it as long as your boat is financed, but once you pay off the loan and set sail, dump the policy! There are very few companies that will insure a blue-water cruise, anyway. Lloyd's may be the only one today. The insurer will make unreasonable demands as a condition of the policy, such as having three experienced crewmen aboard the vessel at all times. And marine insurance for worldwide coverage costs an arm and a leg, assuming you can find it and qualify. A one-year policy for a $50,000 yacht, for example, will cost $3,000 or more.

Taxes. The bureaucrats will have their paws out twice in many jurisdictions: sales or use tax, when you buy the boat, and personal-property tax every year thereafter. Without advocating fraud or getting too involved in complex tax matters here, suffice it to say that you might want to inquire into the possibilities of consummating the boat purchase in another state or even country—one which has a lower sales/use tax or none at all. Another possibility is to purchase the boat for delivery in another state or country. This may require a change of residency or other legal game playing but could qualify the purchase as an interstate or international transaction and, thus, immune from local taxation. On a $40,000 vessel purchased in California, for example, this could mean a savings of $2,400. Your broker should be aware of the possibilities and problems involved.

Personal-property taxes can also get quite expensive. Again, consult with a specialist. Once you leave on your new life, of course, it will be pretty hard for the local taxman to put the bite on you. And after a period of time, you may be exempt—even if you do maintain your legal residence—due to the absence of the boat from their jurisdiction. And then there are always the questionable practices involving playing games with registration in states or countries having lower or no property taxes on vessels: There are an awful lot of expensive yachts berthed in California but registered in Oregon.

Part 4
The Final Stage

12

Equipment and Supplies

A man is rich in proportion to the number of things he can afford to let alone.

Before you reach that day when you can at last set sail for the far horizon, you must be sure that your boat is properly equipped to deal with the seas and filled with sufficient supplies to make life afloat safe and pleasant. This will mean taking a quick inventory of the equipment aboard the boat, assessing its condition, and determining whether additional equipment is needed. If more gear is needed, it must be bought, installed, and tried out before the cruise gets under way; finding out on your first day at sea that the self-steering mechanism does not work can be depressing, to say the least. At the same time, the supplies—food, galley gear, clothing, medical equipment, repair gear, and spare parts—must be purchased, stored aboard the boat, and carefully inventoried.

The equipment will, of course, vary from boat to boat. But the following gear will be found aboard most blue-water vessels:

Engine	Fuel tanks and lines
Head	Dinghy
Transmitter-receiver	Self-steering mechanism
Emergency life raft	Compass

Barometer

Bilge pump

Chronometer

Stove

Depth finder

Water tanks, pump, and lines

Knotmeter or log (or,
preferably, both)

Anchors and line

Sails

Windlass

Winches

Lamps/lights

Sail running gear—
sheets, halyards

142

Each and every bit of this equipment should be carefully inspected and, if it has not recently been tried out, tested. If any gear that is needed has not yet been obtained, it should be bought, installed, and operated under running conditions. The manuals, spare parts list, and warranties for as much of this equipment as possible should be kept aboard in a safe, dry place. In short, before starting the voyage, the skipper should feel confident that all necessary and desired equipment is installed and functional.

Of one thing the skipper can be very sure: Every bit of equipment aboard will eventually malfunction or fail. The ocean offers a very harsh environment for mechanical gizmos; the salt water and sea air are quite corrosive, the constant motion of the boat will cause problems, and the dampness will result in mildew and rot. Therefore, a properly equipped boat will have two things—a satisfactory tool kit and a complete set of spare parts.

The sailor's tool kit is actually a number of tool kits, each designed for a specific type of job: the sail repair kit, the electrical kit, the carpenter's box, the rigging locker, the pump repair kit, the engine repair gear, and the bosun's locker. To simplify things, we'll break it down into two units: the tool chest (electrical, metalwork, pump repair, engine repair, and carpentry) and the sailor's kit (sail repair, rigging, and bosun work). The following represents a suggested set of repair gear for an extended cruise. It must be realized, however, that the lists should not be considered all-inclusive; your own boat and personal needs will vary.

The Tool Chest

Toolbox (non-corrosive,
such as plastic)

Assorted nails, wood
screws, metal screws,
washers, bolts, and nuts

Motor oil

Lubricating oil

Silicone spray lubricant

Wood saw

Hammer

Multipurpose file

Rat-tailed file

Drill and bits

Utility knife

Ignition file

Spark plug gauge

Fiberglass repair kit
Epoxy glue (including
    underwater-setting epoxy)
Cork plugs (various sizes)
Soldering iron (heatable, non-
    electric)
Propane torch
Crowbar
Sledge hammer
Wood hatchet
Wood plane
Assorted pieces of wood
    (for repairs)
1/2″ plywood (for emergency
    hull patching)
3/16″ galvanized telephone
    wire (for repairs and general use)
Hacksaw

Spark plug wrench
Socket wrench set
Allen wrench set
Adjustable crescent wrench
Open-end wrench set
Pipe wrench
Sandpaper
Screwdriver set (insulated)
Pliers
Locking-grip pliers
Needle-nose pliers
Cable cutters
Electrical wire and seizing
Electrical tape
Electrical wire
Portable vise
C-clamp
Tape measure

143

The Sailor's Kit

Ditty bag
Sail needles
Sail tape (waterproof)
Marline
Beeswax
Seizing wire
Thread
Whipping cord
Plastic sealant
Waxed twine
Ripstop tape
Sail patches
Palm
Rigging knife

Shackles (various)
Sail shackles
Turnbuckle toggles
Turnbuckles
Clevis pins
Cotter pins
Pusher (for splicing)
Fids (various)
Nylon tubing
Chafing gear (elkhide)
Rings
Thimbles
Sail slides
Jib hanks

Having these two tool chests aboard will permit the skipper to repair most things that can, and will, go wrong aboard his boat. But what about gear that cannot be repaired, that requires replacement? Again, a relatively complete set of replacement parts for important equipment must be brought along on the voyage. The following is an example of general spare parts that should be carried aboard.

Anchor
Chain
Sails

Running lights
12-volt battery
Flashlight batteries

Propeller
Lines (various)
Burner for stove
Toilet parts
Parts for every pump aboard
  (head, galley, bilge, etc.)
Hand-operated bilge pump
Hose clamps (stainless)
Hose (flexible plastic)

Light bulbs (various)
Fuses (various)
Jumper cable
Tiller
Blocks
Shackles
Winch handles
Battens
Radar reflector

In addition, parts for each important piece of gear should be carried. If, for example, you have a wind vane, a back-up unit or a complete set of parts should be available for this critical piece of gear. If the boat is equipped with a diesel engine, carry the following: oil filter, fuel filter, belts, gaskets, fuel pump, diaphragm, fuel injector, engine valve seals, water pump parts, and thermostat. If a gasoline engine is present, stock up on filters, spark plugs, distributor cap, distributor coil, condenser, breaker points, rotor, generator belt, fuel pump parts (including diaphragm, check valves and gaskets), water pump parts, and various sizes of gaskets.

So much for the basic gear, repair kits, and replacement parts; next step is to check over the navigation inventory. Assuming you will be making blue-water passages, the following books and instruments will be necessary:

Sextant (metal)
Chronometer
Radio receiver (for time checks)
Compass (fixed)
Compass (hand-held)
Radio direction finder (RDF)
Fathometer or lead line
Pilot books
Pilot charts
HO (Hydrographic Office) book
  (for celestial system used)

Nautical almanac
Celestial worksheets
Plotting sheets (with
  compass rose)
Pencils and sharpeners
Set of parallels
Plotting compass
Tide tables
Light lists
Local cruising guides

It is best if the navigational equipment is stored in one area, preferably an area containing a table that can be used for computations and course plotting and that will remain dry.

Another item that more and more cruising sailors are carrying now is a firearm or two. Hijacking on the high seas has become a common phenomenon recently, and boarding by thieves in harbors an almost everyday occurrence in some parts of the world. Some sailors use their guns to hunt animals ashore, supplying the ship's table with fresh meat. At the same time, it must be recognized that carrying guns can cause problems with governmental officials of many countries: The weapons may be temporarily confiscated or at least cause the skipper to fill out additional paperwork. In no event should you ever fail to declare them to the boarding officials. Weighing the pros and cons—and possession of guns is a source of constant argument among cruising sailors—you will probably opt for buying a weapon or two. Advice: Avoid handguns. Many officials can understand your having a rifle but feel that a pistol is concealable and used only against other men. Suggestion: Buy a pump-action 12-gauge shotgun, such as the tried-and-true Remington model 800. This is excellent for hunting and self-defense. Some sailors also carry a rifle—either a small .22 caliber or a larger bore such as .30—.30. A rifle is better suited to hunting game such as deer or wild pig.

Be careful to keep the weapon(s) well lubricated; they can rust quickly at sea. And, of course, bring along sufficient ammunition for your anticipated needs.

Medical and dental equipment is next on the checklist. You may be fortunate enough to be in a modern harbor when that toothache or broken arm happens, but you may also be in the middle of an ocean or anchored in some remote coral atoll. Let's hope that you have prepared yourself by taking first-aid classes and have stocked your sea-going library with Eastman's *Advanced First Aid Afloat* and/or Leone's and Phillips' *The Cruising Sailor's Medical Guide*. In any event, your medical locker should include such nonprescription items as the following:

Seasick pills	Gauze pads (various sizes)
Laxative	Gauze bandage (various sizes)
Antidiarrhea medicine	Absorbent cotton
Antacid	Antiseptic pads
Aspirin	Elastic bandages
Alcohol	Astringent wet dressing
Hydrogen peroxide	Smelling salts
Sun-tan lotion	Skin lotion
Sun-screen lotion	Eye lotion
Sun-screen cream	Thermometer
Burn cream	Hot water bottle
Vasoline petroleum jelly	Tweezers
Antibacterial ointment	Scalpels (two or three sizes)
Adhesive tape (various sizes)	Dental tools (various)
Surgical tape	Syringe and needles
Scissors	Splints
Eye pad	Suture material

In addition to these, you should consult with your family physician and explain that you will be out of touch with any medical facilities for much of the coming years. Ask him to recommend—and give you prescriptions for—other drugs and medicines. Included among these should be pain killers such as novacaine and morphine, stimulants such as amphetamines (there may come a time when your life will depend upon staying awake), sleeping potions such as barbiturates, ointments for preventing infections, medicines for combatting various illnesses, and so on. He may also be helpful in pointing you toward a medical supply store where you can buy basic surgical and dental tools.

146

Your own clothing and that of your family should not be overlooked in conducting an inventory of the boat's equipment and supplies. Not having proper clothing for local conditions can prove not only uncomfortable but dangerous. Again, the list that follows is offered only as an example. Your own will reflect your personal tastes and the demands of geographic areas you expect to visit.

Foul-weather pants	Windbreaker
Foul-weather jacket	Lightweight sweater
Foul-weather boots	One set of lightweight dress
Deck shoes (nonskid)	clothes (for shore)
Working gloves	Heavy, oiled sweater
Wide-brimmed hat	Heavy coat or jacket
Sunglasses (very dark	Wool cap
and polarized)	Thermal underwear
Bathing suit	Socks
Bermuda shorts	Heavy wool shirt
Underwear	Heavy wool trousers
Lightweight cotton pants	Wool gloves
Lightweight cotton shirt/blouse	

You will note the recurrent use of wool. Although itchy, wool has the valuable asset of holding in body heat even when it gets wet—unlike cotton or synthetic materials.

The galley should be carefully stocked and inventoried next. This is going to take some time—some thoughtful planning, extensive shopping, and painstaking storage. Do not make the mistake of trying to "overplan"—that is, work out the menu for every meal over the first six months. You can never tell under what conditions the meal will take place—storm or peaceful haven—and you can never tell when you might land a beautiful mahi-mahi. Anyway, rigid planning takes much of the fun out of cooking and eating.

Still, you are going to have to plan generally in drawing up your list of food stores. In doing this, bear in mind certain considerations.

The item of food should keep fairly well, unless you plan on eating it in the first few days at sea. It should not be too bulky, taking valuable space aboard the boat. It should add to the variety of the diet, while also ensuring that nutritional needs will be met. And it should reflect the individual tastes of the crew members; food can have a disproportionately heavy effect on the morale of sailors after a long stretch at sea.

Provisioning is a matter of taste, of course, and the type and amount of food taken on board will be determined by the anticipated length of the voyage, the possibilities of reprovisioning at future ports, the available storage space aboard and the number of mouths to feed. The presence, type, and capacity of refrigeration is also a factor to consider.

While fresh meat, vegetables, and fruit are always welcome, the skipper should plan on stocking a large supply of food that will not only last but supply energy and be easily consumed. These food items can be lifesavers in emergency conditions, during stormy seas when cooking is nearly impossible or when other food has run out unexpectedly or spoiled. These items include nuts, raisins, dried fruits, honey, granola, beef jerky, pemmican, and tropical chocolate bars. (Again, the following is only an example of a galley's provisions.)

Galley gear

Sponges
Towels
Aluminum foil
Plastic wrap and food bags
Cleanser

Disinfectant
Detergent
Garbage bags
Plastic bucket
Plastic pot scrubbers

Galley staples

Salt (iodized)
Pepper
Vinegar
Soy sauce
Mustard
Sugar
Honey
Salad dressings (packaged)
Peanut butter
Margarine
Ketchup
Coffee
Cream (powdered)
Rice

Milk (condensed or powdered)
Tea
Cocoa mix
Jams and jellies
Garlic
Onions
Lemon juice
Lime juice
Flour
Baking soda
Biscuit mix
Olive oil
Oatmeal

Potatoes
Tomatoes
Brown bread
Minced clams
Bacon
Boned chicken
Boned turkey
Crab
Cheese

Mashed potatoes (powdered)
Mayonnaise
Soup (powdered)
Noodles
Eggs (powdered)
Tabasco
Miscellaneous spices
   and seasonings

148

Canned food

Fruit and vegetable juices
Fruit (pineapple, pears, etc.)
Vegetables (peas, corn, etc.)
Condensed milk
Tuna

Tomato sauce/paste
Beans
Beef stew
Mushrooms
Hash

Fresh provisions

Onions
Potatoes
Bread
Eggs (covered with vaseline)
Fruit (apples, lemons,

   bananas, etc.)
Vegetables (carrots,
   tomatoes, etc.)
Cabbage
Lettuce

There are, of course, hundreds of other possibilities. Freeze-dried meat, fruit, and vegetables are well-suited to life at sea, as they last indefinitely and take up little room. Unfortunately, they are rather expensive and can use up valuable water in restoring them to an edible state. Grinding your own grains aboard ship is another practice that lends itself to cruising. Whole hard winter wheat can be purchased more cheaply than flour and will last longer. Yet another practice that makes life at the ship's table more pleasant is taking aboard mung beans or alfalfa seeds and raising sprouts while sailing; there is nothing so good as fresh green vegetables after several weeks at sea.

Having disposed of food, clothing, and medical supplies, you will be nearing the end of your inventory. And you will be properly amazed at how this mass of equipment and supplies will fit into the limited space of the sailboat. But fit it does; the modern cruising sailboat is a product of ingenious design.

The final checklist will include such items as books, musical instruments, fuel for the engine (diesel or gasoline), fuel for the stove, lamps and heater (alcohol, kerosene, propane, or butane), linen, and water.

The boat is ready.

13

Red Tape

Our life is frittered away by detail . . . . Simplify, simplify.

The bureaucrats are not going to let you out of their grasp completely, of course, It pains them to see a free spirit out there, riding the winds across miles of open ocean, choosing his next temporary home as the mood suits. And so they are going to load you down with paperwork—lots of it. The best thing to do is simply accept it. Understand it for what it is, realize that there is no way out of it—that it is an unpleasant requirement of cruising but a requirement which can be satisfied with a minimal amount of time and effort.

The following is a summary of paperwork that will either be required by law or prove beneficial to you while cruising:

1. Certificate of registry or documentation
2. Radio license
3. Copies of mortgages or liens against the boat
4. Insurance policies
5. Crew lists
6. Passports and visas
7. Entry and clearance papers
8. Medical certificates of health and inoculation
9. Medical records

10. Equipment records, manuals, and warranties
11. Receipts for recent purchases
12. Cash, traveler's checks, foreign currency, letter of credit, etc.

Quite a list—and not exhaustive. Activities such as working ashore in a foreign country or chartering the vessel will require quite a bit more paperwork. But for the average cruising sailor, the list should be complete. Some things, such as insurance and copies of liens, may be inapplicable to your situation.

150

Let's take this flood of paper a bit at a time.

Registration or documentation. A skipper will obtain a certificate of *registration* from the state in which he was a resident when he purchased the vessel. This is much like an automobile registration certificate; it affords proof of title and describes the vessel, while at the same time lining you up to pay the state its required annual fees and personal-property taxes. It should be noted that so long as you remain legally a resident of your state you will be liable for those fees and taxes, regardless of whether you are anchored in that state or in Tahiti. And you must be registered in some state; port authorities will not permit you to enter their country without some valid form showing title to, and nationality of, the vessel.

Documentation is an alternative to registration. Documentation is, basically, registration as a federal vessel—i.e., a vessel registered by the United States rather than by a state. Only vessels of a minimum tonnage (very roughly, the size of a thirty-foot sailboat) can qualify. The home port must be listed as one of the recognized major ports of the U.S.—New York, San Francisco, Norfolk, etc. Documentation does not, however, automatically exempt you from your state's fees and taxes; the same fees and taxes must be paid regardless of whether you are federally documented or state registered—in addition to the documentation fee.

What are the benefits of documentation then? The U.S. Customs Regulations provide that a documented vessel that is not engaged in any trade may proceed from port to port within the United States and its territories without clearing or being subject to boarding upon entry, provided that it has not visited a foreign port or a "hovering vessel." Another possible "advantage" is that some yachtsmen have found ways to elude the taxman through federal documentation—though not legally. Additionally, there appears to be some prestige attached to a documented vessel in foreign waters: The local authorities, it is felt by some yachtsmen, are more reluctant to deal harshly with a U.S. "flag" vessel than they would be with, say, a Florida vessel. This attitude is increasingly less true as the distinctions between documentation and registration disappear.

One misconception many skippers of U.S. flag vessels have is that their exemption from leaving or entering American ports without clearing customs applies to foreign ports as well. Not so! Documentation alters in no way your obligation to clear customs and other agencies of foreign governments. Failure to do this can result in seizure of the vessel and a fine—or even imprisonment.

Another potential problem to be aware of is the possibility of double taxation. Most states and nations have some variation of a rule that considers you a resident if you or your vessel has been within territorial waters for at least six months. Regardless of documentation or registration, hanging around an idyllic island for six months could result in paying that government their required fees and taxes—as well as, possibly, an import duty!

One final note: The documentation or registration number should be carved into a brace or other structure permanently attached to the hull. Although the papers describe the vessel's length, breadth, tonnage, etc., many government officials require the vessel to bear the number in a permanent place.

Radio license. Within U.S. territorial waters, and in the waters of many other nations, possession and/or use of a radio transmitter requires a license. In addition to a license for the radio itself—which may have to be prominently displayed—the person operating the radio may have to be licensed. These regulations are most commonly encountered in the United States, but since you will probably be leaving from the U.S. and periodically returning, a license for the radio should be obtained. As for the operator's license, quite frankly you will probably never be checked. But, of course, you should not operate a transmitter without being familiar with the international rules and terminology.

Copies of mortgages or liens against the boat. If you do not own the boat free and clear, your registration may reflect this. In any event, you should always carry copies of any mortgages or liens currently held against the vessel. Foreign, as well as American, officials can be very sticky about this.

Insurance policies. The true "get away from it all" skipper will say to hell with the blood-sucking insurance companies and take his chances at sea. Rather than betting he will eventually rack his boat up

151

on a reef, he is putting his money on his own abilities as a seaman. Nevertheless, many of you will want to insure your vessel against possible damage or loss. Obtaining marine insurance, by the way, has become increasingly difficult. In many cases, no company but Lloyd's will insure a sailing vessel on a deep-water cruise; if insurance can be found, it will be frighteningly expensive and carry with it restrictive covenants, such as requiring the presence of a minimum number of "qualified" sailors aboard at all times. But if you decide to get insurance (and if the boat carries a mortgage or a lien you will have to) then be sure to carry copies of the policy.

Health insurance is an equally ridiculous—and expensive—thing to have for your new cruising lifestyle. Quite simply, there are no good, full-service health insurance policies with worldwide coverage. Again, Lloyd's comes closest—but at a prohibitive cost.

Crew lists. The governments of most nations require the skipper of a visiting yacht to supply a "crew list" as a part of the customs-clearance procedures. This is simply a list of everyone aboard the vessel, including wife and children, along with their nationality and their status as either working crew or passenger. It is generally best to list them as crew, avoiding the extra paperwork that sometimes comes with the presumption that you are carrying passengers for hire.

Each nation differs as to its exact requirements, but you can count on having to supply multiple copies of the crew list; the U.S. authorities require between four and eight copies of the list for their various agencies. The contents of such lists are relatively uniform, and they can, therefore, often be prepared by the skipper in advance. The list should include the name of the boat, a brief physical description (e.g., two-masted wooden sailing vessel), country of registry, documentation or registration number, gross and net tonnage, last port of call, and date of departure from that port. Then the full name of each person aboard should be listed, along with his or her sex, date and country of birth, nationality, passport number, and status as crew or passenger. The list should be clearly set out in block letters, listing the crew alphabetically.

Passports and visas. It should go without saying that you and your crew have your currently valid passports with you aboard ship and that any visas required of countries you plan to visit in the near future have been obtained.

Entry and clearance papers. The skipper will fly the yellow quarantine flag upon sailing into a country's port of entry and will make no attempt to go ashore. Eventually, the inevitable officials—

customs, immigration, military and/or police—will come aboard, probably wearing hard-heeled boots to mar your decks.

Depending upon the country, some of the following (and possibly more) may be required: customs forms, crew list, stores list (particularly any alcohol, medicines, or firearms), passports, visas, medical certificates, clearance papers from the last port, certificate of registration or documentation, copies of mortgages or liens, radio license, and an itinerary showing date of arrival and departure for every foreign port previously visited. For this last requirement, a ship's log is invaluable. A log should always be kept in any event, as this is *prima facie* evidence of where you have been. Every significant event should be recorded, including the names of officials who board your vessel. Never erase any entry—draw a line through it instead. Never tear a sheet from the log. The apparent accuracy of the ship's log can be critical some day.

153

Once you have cleared the maze of red tape and paid any insidious "fees," you will probably be issued entry papers. Basically, these are permits to cruise the waters of the nation for a limited period of time. These should be kept aboard at all times and shown to officials of other ports you visit. Upon leaving the country, clearance papers should be obtained from the bureaucrats at the last port you visit; these may be required at your next port of entry.

A word should be said about a nasty practice that is developing in some countries, notably in Tahiti. Because of sailing "bums" who have ruined things for others by arriving on the country's shores with dreams of paradise and absolutely no money, government officials are beginning to require skippers to post a cash bond as a condition for being granted entry papers. This bond is commonly in the amount of a one-way airplane ticket home for each and every person aboard the vessel. This can prove at least temporarily expensive but appears to be a practice that is starting to spread to other countries tired of destitute beachcomber types.

Medical certificates of health and inoculation. Some countries require each individual aboard the boat to produce a certificate of health. More commonly, a certificate of recent inoculation against such communicable diseases as smallpox and typhoid fever is necessary. Of course, you and your family will have already taken that precaution; be sure you have the certificates.

Medical records. It is a wise idea to obtain a copy of your personal medical records and those for your family from your physician. It makes it a lot easier for a doctor in a foreign port to treat one of you if he knows your medical history, allergies, etc.

Equipment records, manuals, and warranties. For every significant piece of sophisticated equipment aboard your sailboat, you should have a manual for its operation, maintenance, and repair. This includes the galley stove, head, refrigeration unit, hot and pressurized water systems, depth finder, knotmeter, log, engine, generator, life raft, self-steering mechanism, power windlass—to name but a few common gizmos. This will come in very handy when a piece of equipment breaks down in some foreign port and the local mechanics have never seen or heard of it before. The manual makes it easier to work on the equipment and easier to order, or make, replacement parts. In addition to manuals, records of maintenance and repair should be kept on the major units—engine, generator, depth finder, etc. And any applicable warranties should, of course, be kept aboard.

Receipts for recent purchases. If you have any valuable equipment or personal possessions aboard the boat that appear to have been purchased relatively recently (say, within the past year) you should keep the sales slip. If you do not, you may find yourself paying taxes or customs duties on the object.

Cash, traveler's checks, foreign currency, letters of credit. You will, of course, need money during your voyaging. How should this be kept and in what form? First, you should consider the regulations of countries you intend to visit; most of them will restrict the amount and type of currency that can be brought in or taken out. Second, safety is a factor: If the ship goes down, or is stolen, or you are robbed, you do not want to be instantly destitute. Third, convertibility: You want a form and source of money that will permit you to buy the local currency. Fourth, inflation-proofing: If possible, your money should not be losing ground where it sits.

Each individual will work out his own methods for dealing with money on a blue-water voyage. Perhaps the best approach, however, is a balanced one. Certainly, the greater portion of your savings should be in some type of money-fund account, earning an interest equal to inflationary rates. For the cynic or the super-cautious, a Swiss, Belgian, or Bahamian account may be the answer. But be sure you have made arrangements for the ready transfer of funds to you anywhere in the world. This can often be accomplished with a *letter of credit* from your bank or money-fund organization—a written authorization of credit to you up to a certain amount, with funds transferred to the local bank upon request. Such a document may have beneficial secondary effects as well, establishing your financial solidity in the eyes of suspicious government officials.

But suppose you need money today? Suppose the only bank on the island does not have communications or credit arrangements with foreign banks? Then you had better have some readily convertible form of money. Traveler's checks offer a good solution, particularly if you can buy them during periodic "sales" where the 1 percent commission is reduced by half. Cook's and American Express are universally recognized; Cook's are often less expensive to buy.

And what if there are no banks at all and no places to cash traveler's checks? What if you arrive on a Sunday and everything is closed? Then it's not a bad idea to carry a couple of hundred dollars in U.S. greenbacks socked away somewhere in the boat. Such currency, kept in ones and tens, are often negotiable and can prove handy when nothing but hard cash will do.

Finally, you should try to obtain some of the local currency of the country you expect to visit next. This can often be done at the banks or exchange bureaus of the country you are about to leave. Again, this can come in handy when you arrive in a new country and cannot readily obtain local currency.

14

Where To?

The world is but canvas to our imaginations.

The success of your life afloat will depend to a great degree upon the quality of your sailboat and upon your knowledge and acquired skills. But it will also depend in very great measure upon the elements—winds, currents, doldrums, gales, icebergs, fog, hurricanes. To the extent that these elements can be predicted and planned for, then, the chances of success are appreciably increased. And they can be—to a considerable degree.

It is, of course, a whole lot of fun to sit down at the kitchen table and pore over dozens of charts and guides for far-off romantic places, dreaming about the tropical islands that will be visited once you have saved enough to begin your new life at sea. But it is more than fun; it is a critical step in the planning and execution of a successful long-distance cruise. For without such carefully thought-out long-term planning, the voyage becomes just a crap-shoot, a gamble with nature, with the odds stacked against the sailor.

The planning of your first year or two at sea, then, should be done in the months before you leave harbor. For it will take many, many hours to assimilate the available data on oceanographic and meteorological conditions and coordinate that with projected courses and layover times.

Fortunately, the sailor is blessed with two instruments that make long-term cruising something more than a one-sided guessing game: *Ocean Passages for the World* and pilot charts. And once the long-term plans are made, the short-term courses can be planned with two more invaluable tools: navigational charts and coastal pilots.

Ocean Passages for the World is a large blue book published by the British Navy. First printed in 1895, and revised periodically since then, *Ocean Passages* offers a clear description of the winds, currents, and weather conditions prevailing in any part of any ocean. At the same time, it has text and charts setting forth details of the best routes between almost all significant points of departure and arrival—the best for sailing vessels and the best for powerboats.

The pilot charts are equally valuable. These are individual charts published by the U.S. Navy's Hydrographic Office. The charts use a clever system of symbols and colors to indicate the average strength and direction of both the winds and currents for a given segment of an ocean, as well as the percentage of gales and calms that have been encountered for that area. Each chart represents a certain time period for a specific ocean body. The North Atlantic, for example, is covered by separate charts for each month; the February chart will represent wind and current conditions prevailing in the past over any portion of the North Atlantic in February. The South Pacific, on the other hand, is represented by quarterly charts; a chart will show conditions prevailing there between December and February, for example. These charts are based upon literally millions of observations by mariners over the years and are relatively accurate as to *averages*.

No matter what the average prevailing weather conditions in a given area, of course, there is no guarantee that the sailor will not meet contrary conditions. All this long-term planning is designed to do, then, is to play the averages—to change the odds in favor of the shooter from being in favor of the house. Working on past large-scale observations, the planner can at least maximize his chances of encountering favorable trade winds and currents, and minimize the possibilities of storms, calms, fog, and contrary winds and currents.

Let's see how all this long-distance charting works in practice. We are planning to begin our new life next year by leaving San Francisco for Fiji. What is the best route to take? When should we leave?

Take a look at *Ocean Passages* first for the larger picture. The chart of the world for sailing vessels (found in the back of the book) shows one commonly followed path to Fiji; there are no dates, so the route has apparently been used year round. This tells us only that this course has been much traveled by sailors in the past and is therefore presumably a favorable course. The chart of the general surface current for the world indicates favorable currents prevailing over most of our course: The North Pacific and California currents will sweep us south and west into the stronger North Equatorial Current, which will continue west; the Equatorial Counter Current will give us trouble for a couple of hundred miles or so, but then the South Equatorial Current should take over and again carry us westward in to Fiji. Replacing the *Ocean Passages* charts, we read the text. After looking up "San Francisco" and matching it with "Fiji," we learn that "a track passing east of Takelau Islands, through about 10° 30' S, 171° 00' W and keeping to the great circles, subject to navigational hazards, is recommended for each route."

All right. We have a very general idea now. The currents appear to be favorable year round, pushing us south and then west. A fairly direct route has been followed by thousands of sailors in the past, apparently with few ill effects. And the book recommends a specific course to follow. But when is the best time to leave? What are conditions going to be like along the course for different times of the year?

We turn now to the invaluable pilot charts, both the North Pacific and South Pacific versions. These charts are divided into rectangles of 5°, with a figure in the center of each consisting of a number in a small blue circle, surrounded by blue feathered arrows. The number indicates the percentage of calms or light, variable winds that has been observed within that square for the month or quarter represented by the chart. The blue arrows indicate the average direction and force of the wind from the eight compass points for the square; the length of the arrow represents the percentage of wind from that compass point, while the number of feathers shows the average strength of the wind. Looking at one of the squares, for example, we find that in April there are normally light or no winds 3 percent of the time and that of the remaining 97 percent approximately 60 percent is westerly, 22 percent is northwesterly, 12 percent is southwesterly, and 3 percent is southerly. The prevailing westerly winds, the figure continues to tell us, average about 16 knots, while the other wind directions have run between 8 and 16 knots.

Looking at a small inset chart on the map, we find that 2 percent of all reports for the area during that time period included observations of a gale, i.e., winds in excess of force 8 on the Beaufort Scale.

There are also green arrows, reddish orange solid lines, and dotted blue lines running through the black squares. The green arrows represent prevailing currents; the green numbers next to them show the average speed of the current for the time period. The solid reddish orange lines indicate the path of some of the storms in the past; the numbers show the positions of the storm at Greenwich noon. The dotted blue line represents the percentage of fog for the area, and the other red line shows the minimum and maximum limits of ice and icebergs.

Altogether, extremely valuable information. After using *Ocean Passages* and particularly the pilot charts, it would be difficult to imagine planning a long voyage without them—at least, not safely. With these two tools, you now know not only the general conditions normally prevailing for the oceans you will be crossing and a recommended course for that voyage, but you also know the prevailing wind, weather, and currents for each segment of that trip and for each month or quarter of the year. Again, these are averages; there is no guarantee you will meet idyllic 16 knot westerly trades in a square just because they normally blow that way 95 percent of the time. But at least you have tipped the odds heavily in your favor of maximizing favorable conditions and minimizing the risks and unpleasantness of bad ones. And that can make or break a voyage.

Aboard a bareboat charter in the Vava'n Islands. (*South Pacific Yacht Charters*).

Using these materials, then, you can plan your first leg—to Fiji. You will find the best course and the best time of year to leave. But where next?

You will find that even longer-range planning is necessary if you want to avoid storms and take advantage of good winds and currents. Of course, you do not want to tie yourself down to a rigid schedule; that is one of the things you are trying to get away from. But you should have at least a loose plan in your head of where you intend to travel for the next year or so, based upon consultations with the pilot charts and *Ocean Passages*. The reason is simple: avoiding nasty weather conditions. You will find that various parts of the world have seasonal storms that would make life aboard miserable if not downright dangerous; in others, there is a seasonal shift of winds in a direction directly against your intended course. The monsoons of Asia, for example, result in southwest winds in the Indian Ocean and China Sea from May to September, northeast from October to March. If you do not plan out your voyages long in advance, you may find yourself sitting on a small island for a half year, waiting until the season changes in the area where you next intend to cruise. Loosely planning a year or two ahead, however, permits you to take a larger view of things and to make allowances for prevailing conditions: You can coordinate legs of the trip in such a way as to avoid bad weather. You may wish to visit Samoa immediately, for example; looking six months ahead, however, you may realize that you would not be able to pass through the Torres Straits in time to avoid the foul weather, or perhaps you would encounter still airs even further down the line in the Indian Ocean, or run into gales a year from now in the South Atlantic.

So much for long-term planning for ocean passages. The key is to plan on being in the right place at the right time. What about short-term planning?

Having projected the course of your voyage to take advantage of prevailing weather and oceanic conditions, you must then prepare yourself for what is sometimes referred to as *coastal piloting*. This simply means navigation at sea but within a day's sail of land. In other words, you should prepare yourself for dealing with more precise planning once you leave the relative safety of the open seas and approach the potential dangers of landfall. For this, you will principally need navigational charts; coastal pilots and local guidebooks are also helpful.

Navigational charts are self-explanatory. Assuming you have properly prepared yourself for your new life at sea, you will have taken a course or two in navigation—celestial and coastal—and will be familiar with the use of charts. You will also realize how very critical they are to the success and safety of a voyage. Quite simply, one is lost without them.

The charts come in different scales, of course. The large-scale charts of a large area or even entire ocean are helpful in charting long-term voyages and in recording progress during the voyage. Smaller scale charts will be necessary as you approach land masses, however, and smaller scale yet when dealing with harbors and anchorages. Only

Charter cruising in the Kingdom of Tonga. (*South Pacific Yacht Charters*)

a very small-scale chart is going to show that tiny submerged reef at the entrance to the harbor that could tear the guts out of your boat.

Make sure you have obtained all the charts you think you will need *before* you leave on your voyage. They can be very difficult (in many places, impossible) to obtain once you have set sail. And this is another important reason for carefully plotting out your projected course for the next year or two. There are thousands of charts available covering the oceans of the world. To buy all of them would cost a fortune and would fill the boat cabin. Yet if the charts are not purchased in the U.S. or Canada, they may never be available again. So it becomes necessary to know exactly which charts will be needed, i.e., where you are planning to cruise for the next year or two.

Once sufficient charts have been purchased, including small-scale ones of places you intend to visit, you must fold or roll them, and use some system of ready identification and indexing. This is important, since it may become critical at some time to locate a chart very quickly. Once properly labeled, some system of safe storage should be used.

Coastal pilots are a very helpful tool to the skipper approaching a new landfall. These are books published by the American and British governments that give sailing directions for coastlines and islands all over the world. Each volume deals with a particular country or area and begins by giving some general remarks about navigation in that neck of the woods, including comments concerning how to avoid nasty weather and dangerous currents. The book then discusses the social, economic, and political nature of the country and explains the local rules on right-of-way, buoys, mooring, signals, and so on. The rest of the volume deals with detailed descriptions of the coastlines and harbors, pointing out dangers to watch for and offering suggested directions for anchoring in a harbor, avoiding a reef, running a strait. Landmarks, lights, and unusual land formations are noted for use in navigation.

162

The British Hydrographic Department publishes over seventy volumes of pilots covering most of the navigable world. These are supplemented each year with the latest corrections and additions. The U.S. Coast and Geodetic Survey offers their own, smaller collection of pilot books, which covers the coastlines of the U.S., including Hawaii and Alaska.

Local guidebooks can also be helpful. In fact, in some areas the information contained in them is more current and accurate than the pilot books. When cruising in the Bahamas or the Caribbean, for example, the cruising guidebooks designed for use by private yachts should be purchased and reviewed in advance.

Now you have the tools necessary to make long-range plans for where to go and to navigate your way to a safe anchorage once you get there. You can plan your voyage by considering the oceanographic and meteorological conditions prevalent worldwide. The oceans are, you now realize, a very roughly predictable shifting panorama of winds, currents, storms, ice floes, and hurricanes—and you must adapt your plans to accommodate their average conditions for a given time period. Once you close on your landfall, you can safely deal with the reefs, sand bars, treacherous currents, sunken wrecks, and sudden storms by referring to your charts and pilots.

But where to? Where are the best cruising areas? What is the best route to take if you want to sail around the world?

Of course, what areas make up the best cruising grounds is a subject for considerable disagreement among blue-water sailors. Perhaps you will have already had some sailing experiences, or you have some places you want to visit above all others. Generally, there is some agreement that two broad areas are idyllic for cruising: the Caribbean and the South Pacific. For some, the Mediterranean would be added, particularly the Greek Isles. For others, the Bahamas offer heaven-on-earth. Still others are attracted to Mexico or the San Juan Islands or New Zealand. It is all largely a matter of personal taste—as to climate, sailing conditions, scenery, the native people, the degree of isolation. Certainly, any of the areas mentioned should offer pleasant cruising experiences.

For the round-the-world sailor, a word about prevailing conditions. As a study of *Ocean Passages* and pilot charts will indicate, the heavily preferred way is to make your passage from east to west. If, for example, you are leaving from Ft. Lauderdale, the ideal—and most commonly traveled—course lies through the Caribbean, on into the Pacific by way of the Panama Canal, perhaps stopping off at the Galapagos, and on into the South Pacific—the Marquesas, possibly the dangerous Tuamotus, the Society Islands, Samoa, Fiji. Then on to New Zealand and Australia, through the Torres Straits and into the Indian Ocean; around South Africa, up the Atlantic and back to the Caribbean by running up the Antilles—Barbados, Martinique, Guadalupe, Virgin Islands, etc. Of course, for the really adventurous there are innumerable variations, including taking on the Mt. Everest of cruising, Cape Horn.

There it is. You have seen that it *can* be done. You have been shown how you can afford to retire to a life sailing the oceans of the world. You have read how to select your future floating home, how to prepare both yourself and the boat for a cruising life, how to earn a living at sea, how to give your kids a formal education—and even how to plan where to go.

You know the way.

The rest is up to you.

Bibliography

*How many a man has dated a new era in his life
from the reading of a book.*

How to Sail

Basic Sailing by M. B. George (Hearst Books, 1978)

Better Sailing by Richard Henderson (Contemporary Books, 1977)

Boat Handling by the Library of Boating Service (Time-Life, 1975)

Chapman's Piloting, Seamanship and Small Boat Handling by Charles F. Chapman (Hearst Books, 1976)

Colgate's Basic Sailing Theory by Stephen Colgate (Van Nostrand Reinhold, 1973)

Complete Book of Sailing by Peter Cook and Barbara Webb (Doubleday, 1977)

Encyclopedia of Sailing by the editors of *Yacht Racing-Cruising Magazine* (Harper & Row, 1978)

Fundamentals of Sailing, Cruising and Racing by Stephen Colgate (Norton, 1978)

Good Sailing: An Illustrated Course on Sailing by the editors of *Rudder* (McKay, 1976)

The New Glenans Sailing Manual by Glenans Sea Center (Norton, 1978)

Royce's Sailing Illustrated by Patrick Royce (Western Marine Enterprises, 1979)

Sailing Made Easy by Rufus G. Smith (Dodd, 1952)

Sail Power by Wallace Ross (Knopf, 1975)

Sailing for Beginners by Moulton H. Farnham (Macmillan, 1975)

Successful Sailing by Lou D'Alpuget (Macmillan, 1973)

This is Sailing by Richard Creagh-Osborne (Sail Books, 1973)

Cruising

Blue Water by Robert and Nancy Griffith (Norton, 1979)

Come Aboard by Eric C. Hiscock (Oxford University Press, 1978)

Cruising by J. D. Sleightholme (Beekman, 1973)

Cruising by the Library of Boating Service (Time-Life, 1976)

Cruising as a Way of Life by Thomas E. Colvin (McKay, 1980)

Cruising under Sail by Eric C. Hiscock (Oxford University Press, 1965)

Deep Sea Sailing by Errol Bruce (McKay, 1978)

Go Cruising by Daniel Gilles and Michael Malinovsky (Scribner, 1979)

Handbook of Small Boat Cruising by Fox Green (Time Books, 1974)

Ocean Voyaging by David Parker (DeGraff, 1975)

Sail Far Away: Reflections on Live Afloat by Robert Carter (Norton, 1978)

Sea Sense by Richard Henderson (International Marine, 1979)

Cruising Adventures

Across Three Oceans by Conor O'Brien (DeGraff, 1949)

After 50,000 Miles by Hal Roth (Norton, 1977)

Alone around the World by Naomi James (Coward, 1979)

Around the World Alone by Alain Colas (Barron, 1978)

Atlantic Cruise in Wanderer III by Eric C. Hiscock (Oxford University Press, 1968)

Bibliography

Cruising in Seraffyn by Lin and Larry Pardy (McKay, 1979)

Dove by Robin L. Graham (Bantam, 1978)

Great Adventures in Small Boats by David Klein and Mary L. King (Macmillan, 1963)

Ice by Tristan Jones (Andrews & MacMeel, 1978)

Ice Bird by David Lewis (Norton, 1976)

The Long Way by Bernard Moitessier (Beekman, 1979)

Saga of a Wayward Sailor by Tristan Jones (Andrews & MacMeel, 1979)

Sail before Sunset by Earl Hinz (McKay, 1978)

Sea Quest by Charles Borden (Macrae, 1966)

Seraffyn's European Adventures by Lin and Larry Pardy (Norton, 1979)

Southwest in Wanderer IV by Eric C. Hiscock (Oxford University Press, 1973)

Storm Passage by Webb Chiles (Time Books, 1977)

Survive the Savage Sea by Dougal Robertson (Bantam, 1974)

Trekka around the World by John Guzzwell (DeGraff, 1979)

Two against Cape Horn by Hal Roth (Norton, 1978)

Two on a Big Ocean by Hal Roth (Norton, 1978)

Wandering under Sail by Eric C. Hiscock (Oxford University Press, 1977)

Woman Alone by Clare Francis (McKay, 1980)

Cruising Area Guides

The Adriatic: A Sea Guide to Venice, the Italian Shore, and the Dalmatian Coast by H. M. Denham (Norton, 1977)

The Aegean: A Sea Guide to Its Coast and Islands by H. M. Denham (Norton, 1976)

Boating in Mexico by Dix Brow (Haessner Publishing, 1977)

Cruising Guide to the Bay Islands of Honduras by Julius M. Wilensky (Westcott Cove, 1979)

Cruising Guide to the Caribbean and the Bahamas by Jerrems C. Hart and William T. Stone (Dodd, 1979)

Cruising the Northwest by Donald Holm (Prentice-Hall, 1977)

Cruising the Inland Waterways of Europe by Jarrett and Stanley Kroll (Harper & Row, 1979)

Cruising the San Juan Islands by Bruce Calhoun (Sea Publications, 1973)

Northwest Passages by Bruce Calhoun (Western Marine Enterprises, 1978)

Pacific Islands Yearbook (International Publication Service, 1977)

Sea Guide—Southern California by Leland Lewis (Sea Publications)

Yachtsman's Guide to the Windward Islands edited by Julius M. Wilensky (Westcott Cove, 1978)

Boat and Boat Design

American Small Sailing Craft by Howard Chapelle (Norton, 1951)

Book of Boats by William and John Atkin (International Marine, 1976)

Brewer's Cruising Designs Power and Sail by Edward S. Brewer (McKay, 1979)

The Case for the Cruising Trimaran by Jim Brown (International Marine, 1975)

Colan Archer and the Seaworthy Double Ender by John Leather (International Marine, 1979)

Designer's Notebook by Ian Nicholson (Scribner, 1979)

Evolution of Modern Sailboat Design by M. Gougeon and T. Knog

Ferro Cement: Design, Techniques, Application by Bruce Bingham (Cornell Maritime, 1974)

The Finely Fitted Yacht by Ferenc Mate (Norton, 1979)

Further Offshore by J. H. Illingworth (Scribner, 1979)

Good Boats by Roger C. Taylor (International Marine, 1977)

An L. Francis Herreshoff Reader by L. Francis Herreshoff (International Marine, 1978)

The Ocean Sailing Yacht by Donald M. Street, Jr. (Norton, 1973)

The Proper Yacht by Arthur Beiser (Norton, 1979)

The Sailing Yacht by Juan Baader (Norton, 1979)

Sensible Cruising Designs by L. Francis Herreshoff (International Marine, 1973)

Understanding Boat Designs by Edward S. Brewer and Jim Betts (International Marine, 1971)

Bibliography

Yacht Designs by William Garden (International Marine, 1977)

Navigation

Basic Astro Navigation by Conrad Dixon (Granada, 1977)

Basic Coastal Navigation by Conrad Dixon (Granada, 1977)

Calculator Navigation by Mortimer Rogoff (Norton)

Celestial Navigation by Frances W. Wright (Cornell Maritime, 1974)

Celestial Navigation H.O. 249 by John E.d Milligan (Cornell Maritime, 1974)

Celestial Navigation for Yachtsmen by Mary Blewitt (DeGraff, 1967)

Celestial Navigation Step by Step by Warren Norville (International Marine, 1975)

Coastal Navigation Step by Step by Warren Norville (International Marine, 1975)

Dead Reckoning by C. Northcote Parkinson (Houghton Mifflin, 1978)

Dutton's Navigation and Piloting by G. D. Dunlap and H. H. Shufeldt (Naval Institute Press, 1972)

Marine Navigation by Richard R. Hobbs (Naval Institute Press, 1974)

Nautical Almanac (U.S. Hydrographic Office—yearly)

Navigation by the Library of Boating Service (Time-Life, 1975)

Noon Sight Navigation by A. A. Birney (Cornell Maritime)

Ocean Yacht Navigator by Kenneth Wilkes (McKay, 1976)

Piloting and Dead Reckoning by H. H. Shufeldt and G. D. Dunlap (Naval Institute Press, 1970)

Primer of Navigation by George W. Mixter (Van Nostrand Reinhold, 1967)

Self-Taught Navigation by Robert Y. Kittredge (Northland, 1970)

Yachtsman's Navigation Manual by Jeff E. Tughill (DeGraff, 1976)

Maintenance, Repair, and Marlinspike

The Art of Knotting and Splicing by Cyrus L. Day (Naval Institute Press, 1970)

The Arts of the Sailor by Harvey G. Smith (Barnes & Noble, 1979)

Ashley Book of Knots by Clifford W. Ashley (Doubleday, 1944)

Boat Repairs and Conversions by Michael Verney (International Marine, 1970)

Care and Repair of Hulls by Michael Verney (Scribner, 1979)

Creative Ropecraft by Stuart E. Grainger (Norton, 1979)

The Ditty Bag Book by Frank Rosenow (Norton, 1977)

Engine Maintenance and Repair by David MacLean (Tab Books, 1977)

Fiberglass Repairs by P. J. Petrick (Cornell Maritime, 1976)

Fitting Out by J. D. Sleightholme (Scribner, 1979)

Handbook of Knots by Raoul Graumont (Cornell Maritime, 1945)

Handbook of Practical Boat Repairs by Percy Blandford (Tab Books, 1975)

How to Repair Diesel Engines by Paul Dempsey (Tab Books, 1975)

Knots and Lines Illustrated by Paul and Arthur Synder (DeGraff, 1970)

Maintenance by the Library of Boating Service (Time-Life, 1976)

The Marlinspike Sailor by Hervey G. Smith (DeGraff, 1969)

Modern Marlinspike Seamanship by William P. MacLean (Bobbs-Merrill, 1979)

Modern Rope Seamanship by Colin Jarman and Bill Beavis (International Marine, 1979)

Smallcraft Maintenance by Percy Blanford

Splicing Wire and Fiber Rope by Raoul Graumont and John Hensel (Cornell Maritime, 1945)

Meteorology

Boating Weather: How to Predict It, What to Do About It by Sallie Townsend and Virginia Ericson (McKay, 1978)

Heavy Weather Guide by Edwin T. Harding and William T. Kotsch (Naval Institute Press, 1965)

Heavy Weather Sailing by Adlard Coles (DeGraff, 1975)

Instant Wind Forecasting by Alan Watts (Dodd, 1975)

Yachtsman's Weather Guide by Ingrid Holford (Van Nostrand Reinhold, 1979)

Marine Cooking

Cooking Afloat by Beverley Fuller (McKay Books, 1976)

The Cruising Chef by Michael B. Greenwald (Tab Books, 1977)

Bibliography

The Cruising Cook by Shirley H. Deal (Deal Associates, 1977)

Galley Book by Janet Groene (McKay, 1977)

Galley Cookbook by Gwen Skinner (Reed, 1979)

Heavy Weather Cooking by Jan Silver (International Marine, 1980)

New Cruising Cookbook by Russel Jones and C. McKim (Norton, 1960)

One Burner Cookbook by Harriet Barker (Contemporary Books, 1975)

Starchild's and Holahan's Seafood Cookbook by Adam Starchild and James Holahan (Pacific Search, 1978)

Miscellaneous

Advanced First Aid Afloat by P. F. Eastman (Cornell Maritime, 1974)

Boatbuilding by Howard I. Chappell (Norton, 1941)

Boatbuilding in Your Own Backyard by Samuel S. Rable (Cornell Maritime, 1958)

Boatman's Guide to Light Salvage by George H. Reid (Cornell Maritime, 1979)

The Charter Game: How to Make Money Sailing Your Own Boat by Ross Norgrove (International Marine, 1979)

Chartering and Charter Parties by H. B. Cooley (Cornell Maritime, 1974)

The Cruising Sailors Medical Guide by Nicholas C. Leone (McKay, 1978)

How to Buy a Boat by Bob Whittier (Aztex, 1978)

Oceanography and Seamanship: A Guide for Ocean Cruising by William G. Van Dorn (Dodd, 1974)

Oxford Companion to Ships and Sea by P. K. Kemp (Oxford University Press, 1976)

Sea Survival by Dougal Robertson (Merrimack Book Service)

Self-Steering for Sailboats by Gerard Dijkstra (Sail Books, 1979)

Self-Steering for Sailing Craft by John Letcher (International Marine, 1974)

Surveying Small Craft by Ian Nicholson (International Marine, 1974)

Note: This is, of course, only a partial listing of books available on the indicated subjects. If any on these books cannot be obtained from your local

library, bookstore, or marine supply store, it can be purchased from Bluewater
Books, 109 Mariners Square, 1900 North Northlake Way, Seattle,
Washington, 98103. This bookstore has one of the largest inventories of
marine books to be found anywhere in the world.

Index

174